The Gourmet's Guide to

Northwest Bed & Breakfast Inns

Anne Nisbet

Speed Graphics

"When you wake up in the morning, Pooh,"
said Piglet, "What's the first thing you say to yourself?"
"What's for breakfast?" said Pooh.

A. A. Milne
Winnie the Pooh

*This book is dedicated
to the memory of my mother, Claire Saxton,
with whom I spent many happy hours in the kitchen.*

About the Author

Born in Madrid, Spain to Northwest-native parents, one of Anne Nisbet's first words was "pan" (bread), indicating an early interest in food. By the age of six, Anne had begun her now-extensive cookbook collection which today numbers in the hundreds, with volumes ranging from food history and vintage Fannie Farmer to contemporary best-sellers and menu cookbooks.

Over the years, Anne's passion for food was continually demonstrated; cooking family meals, memorizing the recipe for Toll House cookies by the age of ten, experimenting with seasoning by doctoring Campbell's soups with herbs, preparing veal parmesan for her first dinner party at sixteen and planning parties for friends. Called Martha Child by her family, Anne eventually landed in the food-service industry after graduating from Seattle's Roosevelt High School and the University of Washington.

Her love of food and parties propelled Anne into the catering industry where she has spent the majority of her career. As Catering Director for nationally-known Ray's Boathouse Restaurant, Anne planned thousands of parties both at Ray's and at locations throughout the Puget Sound region. Now an independent consultant and freelance planner, food stylist and author, she puts her talents to use for a broad range of clients.

Anne enjoys good food and good wine, baking, gardening, reading and throwing a great party. A self-proclaimed lavender addict, she grows a dozen varieties of the herb in the garden of her home in Seattle's Magnolia neighborhood. Anne spends her free time cooking or thinking about what to cook next and tries to spend as much time as she can at her family's vacation home on Pebble Beach at Suquamish, Washington.

Copyright © 1998 by Speed Graphics

All rights reserved. No part of this publication may be reproduced by any mechanical, photographic or electronic process or otherwise copied for public or private use without the advance written permission of Chuck Hill, c/o Ballard Bratsberg, Inc., 506 2nd Ave. W., Seattle, WA 98119. Telephone: (206) 284-8800.

Printed in the United States of America
ISBN 0-9617699-9-8

Introduction

I have traveled thousands of miles researching A Gourmet's Guide to Northwest Bed & Breakfast Inns and it has been a rewarding experience. The Northwest is full of glorious scenery, great restaurants, interesting sightseeing and any variety of lodgings. Truth be told, I have often preferred luxury hotels while on holiday. No prejudice, just simply habit, and a desire to have a wealth of amenities at my beck and call. Perhaps it's my years in the catering business, always seeing to others' needs, and wanting the same when I vacationed. Until beginning this project, I wasn't fully aware of the delights that bed and breakfasts present to the traveler.

What sets these inns apart from their hotel/motel brethren is the level of personal service and hospitality unavailable anywhere else, even in five-star properties. With few exceptions, it is the owner/innkeeper who greets you, sees to your needs, cooks and serves you breakfast, offers tips for local touring and helps with reservations. You are a guest in their home and your innkeeper hosts are genuinely interested in your comfort and pleasure. In larger towns and cities, bed and breakfasts are also becoming increasingly popular with business travelers as a much-preferred alternative to sterile and impersonal hotels. The innkeepers I spoke with have all experienced this trend, particularly with women travelling on business, who find B & Bs a more secure environment.

This book is designed to guide you to establishments that will provide you with comfortable lodgings in a variety of settings. These bed and breakfast inns offer a wide array of accommodations, whether luxurious or simple, water view or mountain-top. There is something for everyone and every pocketbook. The other agreeable aspect of these establishments is, of course, the pleasure to be had at the breakfast table.

Few of us take the time to sit in the morning and linger over a tasty meal, opting instead to suck down a drive-through espresso and inhale a muffin while dodging traffic. It is impractical for most to undertake full meal preparations on busy weekdays. Some weekend soon, set aside the time to treat yourself and your family and friends to the luxury of a home-cooked morning meal. Set the table with your favorite china, pick some flowers or herbs from the garden or create a colorful centerpiece with fruit and vegetables. Invest in some top-quality coffee beans, brew a pot of aromatic java and listen to your favorite CDs while preparing a delicious meal.

There are plenty of recipes to choose from, whether you prefer a sweet or savory start to your day. And not all recipes need be prepared for breakfast or brunch. Quick breads, yeast breads, cakes and cookies make for appealing afternoon and evening treats, too. Some of the egg dishes could work very well for a simple dinner. The other advantage is that many of these recipes can be prepared fully or partially in advance, simplifying meal preparation. The innkeepers contributed these recipes, selecting dishes that are particularly popular with their guests, reflect their style of cooking or feature an ingredient specific to their region. Recipes have been tested and edited to present them in a common language and format.

If you are a fan of bed and breakfast inns, I hope you'll find a new destination in this book. If you haven't taken the opportunity to try a bed and breakfast, I hope you will use this book as a guide to a whole new world. Enjoy!

Acknowledgments

Few books are written solely by the author. While the words may be penned by one individual, the stories they tell are inspired by the experiences of many. Certainly that is the case for this book, which could not have been completed without the participation of the innkeepers and their respective establishments featured in this book. My thanks to them, for graciously opening their doors to me and sharing their personal and professional histories - and their recipes!

I am blessed with a wonderful family and great friends who have cheered me along these past months. My thanks to:

My partner, Kurt Krause, for believing I can do anything, your always enthusiastic reviews of my work, and for loving me as much as you do. My sister, Karen Blonden, for your excellent advice and always-willing ear. Colin and Marie Nisbet, for never doubting my decision to leave an established career to pursue an uncharted course. To Rick Blonden, Renee and Tom Holland and Bruce and Lisa Nisbet, for your interest and support. Ginny Morey, reader and writer extraordinaire, for your editorial input. Claudia Kibbee and Tricia Clearman for years of friendship and support. Jacob Kleinman-Krause, for your enthusiastic recipe testing and being the first to request my autograph. Family and friends at Pebble Beach, for your enthusiasm and interest in this project.

My publisher, Chuck Hill, is also most deserving of thanks. I recall a conversation with him, standing in the sunshine outside of Ray's Boathouse, where I commented that someday I hoped to write about food and travel. Thank you for remembering that conversation and giving me the opportunity to realize a dream. I hope you also realize a dream with the publishing of this book.

Credits

Cover photograph courtesy of Marilyn Loewke, Chestnut Hill Inn, Orcas Island, Washington. Photo taken by J. K. Lawrence.

Additional photographs courtesy of Amy's Manor, Mt. Ashland Inn, The Old Farmhouse, Wilp Gybuu, The Purple House, Lighthouse Bed and Breakfast, Ann Starrett Mansion, Home by the Sea, Colonel Crockett Farm, Captain Whidbey Inn and Schnauzer Crossing.

Table of Contents

Bed & Breakfast Inns of British Columbia

The Beaconsfield Inn 13
   Plum & Pineapple Chutney
Heritage Harbour 19
   Cranberry Blueberry Raisin Bread
Laburnam Cottage 23
   Blueberry Coffee Cake
The Old Farmhouse 27
   Vanilla Soufflé, Cheese Blintzes
Penny Farthing Inn 33
   Dutch Butter Cake, Scones
Richview House 37
   Fruit Crepes with French Vanilla Yogurt and Orange Ginger Sauce
Sooke Harbour House 43
   Dutch Babies with Red Huckleberry-Maple Syrup Puree, Oyster Bars
Thistledown House 53
   Birchermuesli, Chocolate Waffles with Bing Cherry Sauce, Rhubarb Pie
Wilp Gybuu 61
   Mediterranean Quiche with Hash Brown Crust

Bed & Breakfast Inns of Oregon

The Campbell House 67
   Campbell House Scones, Hazelnut Chicken Tea Sandwiches
Chanticleer Inn 73
   Northwest Eggs Supreme
Flora's Lake House 77
   Aunt Bobbie's Sticky Bun Cake, Cranberry Muffins
Home by the Sea 83
   Almond Eggnog French Toast
Lighthouse Bed & Breakfast 87
   Shirley's Cheesecake, Blueberry Brunch Casserole
The Lion & the Rose 93
   Banana Sour Cream French Toast
Mattey House 97
   Chicken Liver Pâté
Mount Ashland Inn 101
   Turkey Sausage, Mountain Almond Roca, Fresh Pear Cobbler, Smoked Salmon Spread

Portland Guest House 107
   Pumpkin Waffles with Oregon Hazelnut Butter
Portland's White House 111
   Butter Pecan French Toast, Caramelized Onion and Portobello Frittata
The Romeo Inn 117
   Cranberry Pecan Scones
Rosebriar Hotel 121
   Finnish Pancakes
Sea Quest Bed & Breakfast 125
   Orange Poppyseed Bundt Cake
Springbrook Hazelnut Farm 131
   Hazelnut Granola Parfaits
Steamboat Inn 135
   Salmon Hash with Lemon Dill Yogurt Sauce, Cinnamon Orange
   French Toast with Vanilla Ricotta Filling
Steiger Haus 141
   Kiwi-Banana French Toast
Touvelle House 145
   Breakfast Casserole
Tyee Lodge 151
   Tyee Quiche, Cinnamon Roll Rose

Bed & Breakfast Inns of Washington

Amy's Manor 159
   Pears Simmered in Cider
Ann Starrett Mansion 163
   Rose Petal Jam, Madeira Cake, Madeleines
The Captain Whidbey Inn 171
   Spiced Fruit Compote, Lemon Poppy Seed Bread, Crab Cakes, Granola
The Chambered Nautilus 177
   Rosemary Buttermilk Muffins, Northwest Salmon Breakfast Pie,
   Pumpkin Spice Bread, Stuffed French Toast with Orange Syrup
Channel House 185
   Oatmeal Pancakes with Buttermilk Syrup, Cheese Puff
Chestnut Hill Inn 191
   Apple Pancakes, Homemade Apple Sage Sausage,
   Zucchini Cakes, Chocolate Walnut Tart
The Colonel Crockett Farm 199
   Banana Bran Muffins
Groveland Cottage 203
   Dungeness Crab Quiche, Rogue River Special

The James House 209
Poached Pears with Rhubarb Sauce
Lake Union Bed & Breakfast 215
Lake Union Pancake, Lake Union Eggs Caviar
Olympic Lights 221
Buttermilk Biscuits, Oregano Eggs, Savory Vegetable Torte
The Purple House 227
Apple Raisin Oatmeal
Schnauzer Crossing 231
Apple Amaretto Crêpes, Triple Sec French Toast,
Cascade Mountain Range Muffins with Glacier Topping
The Shelburne Inn 237
Ann's Bread Pudding, Croutons of Asparagus and Crab
Turtleback Farm Inn 243
Smoked Salmon Torte, Warm Chocolate Espresso Pudding Cakes
Waverly Place 249
Swedish Pancakes with Huckleberry Sauce

Index by recipe located on page 262.

British Columbia Bed & Breakfast Inns

The Beaconsfield
Heritage Harbour
Laburnam Cottage
The Old Farmhouse
Penny Farthing Inn
Richview House
Sooke Harbour House
Thistledown House
Wilp Gybuu

The smell of buttered toast simply talked to Toad,
and with no uncertain voice; talked of warm kitchens,
of breakfast on bright frosty mornings, of cosy parlour firesides
on winter evenings, when one's ramble was over and slippered feet were
propped on the fender; of the purring of contented cats,
and the twitter of sleepy canaries.

Kenneth Grahame
The Wind in the Willows

The Beaconsfield Inn

998 Humboldt Street
Victoria, B.C. V8V 2Z8
Canada
Phone (250) 384-4044
Toll Free (888) 884-4044
Fax (250) 384-4052
Website: http://www.islandnet.com/beaconsfield
Email: beaconsfield@islandnet.com

Rates:
High Season: $200 - 350 Canadian
Low Season: $145 - 225 Canadian

The Beaconsfield Inn

In the halcyon days prior to World War I, Edward VII frequented the fashionable Beaconsfield Hotel in London on a regular basis. Legend has it that the son of the ever so straight-laced Queen Victoria enjoyed the hotel as a hideaway for romantic trysts.

Those seeking a romantic retreat today should look to the London hotel's namesake in Victoria, British Columbia. The Beaconsfield Inn was named for Edward's favorite rendezvous with a nod to preserving the same sense of romance and seclusion enjoyed by the king and, one presumes, his guests.

This Beaconsfield was built as a private home in 1905 by one of the provinces' premier architects, Samuel McClure and epitomizes the elegant simplicity in favor at the time. The highly ornamented, Gothic-influenced elements of the Victorian architecture were eschewed, to be replaced with the cleaner, uncomplicated lines of the Arts and Crafts movement. The result was a handsome home, a gift to Gertrude Rithet, from her father, R.P. Rithet, Victoria mogul and onetime mayor.

No doubt Gertrude admired the peacock-inspired stained glass in the sunroom, the rich African mahogany paneling in the entry hall, the eleven-foot high beamed ceilings and the book-lined library. The house exudes luxury, solidity and calm, though this was not always the case. As with many old homes, this one passed through various owners over the years. It became a hospital during WWII, then a nursing home facility. Standing empty for several years, it was rescued from the wrecking ball in the early '80s to be reincarnated as an inn. Significant improvements were made to update the home for guests, but it wasn't until 1993, when Con and Judi Sollid bought the Beaconsfield, that it was restored to its original grandeur.

Arrive at the Beaconsfield mid-afternoon and find tea, in a silver service, awaiting in the library. Sink into the down-cushioned sofa and relish the quiet. The room is once again lined with books and accented with hunting prints. A black leather Chesterfield sofa sits next to the fireplace, sporting velvet and tapestry pillows. One can imagine Edwardian gentlemen gathering here, indulging in  postprandial cigars and brandy, luxuriating in masculine comfort.

Comfort abounds at The Beaconsfield Inn. The guest rooms were designed to pamper the most discriminating of travelers. A split of sparkling wine welcomes guests to each of the six spacious rooms and three glorious suites. Carefully selected antiques and oriental carpets decorate the rooms, complemented by pale colors on the walls along with English country florals and stripes on the soft furnishings . Bring along Henry James and Edith Wharton to read seated before a crackling fire - seven rooms enjoy wood-burning fireplaces, a reminder of the days before central heating. Modern touches include either jetted or built-for-two whirlpool tubs in all the rooms except the Duchess. Here, guests enjoy a relic of wealthy Edwardians' fascination with bathroom furnishings, a rare, wood-canopied tub and shower. At day's end, slip beneath a down-filled duvet to dream of cream teas and croquet played on green lawns.

In the morning, guests help themselves to breakfast from the sideboard in the restored dining room and can dine there, or select a seat in the sunroom. The double-hung window separating the two rooms remains open so guests in the dining room can hear the pleasant sound of the fountain in the white-painted sunroom where black and white parquet flooring sets off floral-cushioned wicker chairs and lush plants. The peacock-colored stained glass still glows, jewel-like, in the big, sunny windows, through which guests can admire the mature trees and well-tended beds on the tidy grounds of Beaconsfield.

THE GOURMET'S GUIDE TO NORTHWEST BED & BREAKFAST INNS

Guests who prefer a stroll after breakfast often enjoy a walk to Beacon Hill Park, just a block away. Victoria's many parks and public gardens provide constant floral displays including the sunken rose garden and lily pond at Government House and the delightful Crystal Garden conservatory where exotic plants, rare tropical birds and butterflies delight with their showy colors and the world's smallest monkeys charm with their antics.

Fifty acres of extravagant landscaping are showcased at Butchart Gardens, one of Victoria's most popular attractions. Home to a Japanese garden, an Italian garden, a rose garden and a sunken garden (created on the site of a depleted limestone quarry), phenomenal floral displays take place each season, drawing devotees back time and again. Ponds and fountains add sparkle to the grounds and music lovers will appreciate concerts on the lawn in summer months.

Victoria is an excellent city in which to walk. Two favorite destinations, flanking the Inner Harbour, are the regal Parliament Buildings and The Empress Hotel, preferred purveyor of English high tea. Shops full of cashmere and wool clothing, English porcelain, toffee and loose tea tempt Anglophiles looking to take home a bit of old England. Visitors thirsty for a taste of old England might duck into one of the many pubs for a quick pint while tossing a dart or two. Refreshed, head to the Royal British Columbia Museum to learn about the Island's natural history and peoples through creative exhibits featuring the recreation of a 20th century frontier town, an Indian village and an old-growth rain forest.

After a busy day, return to the sanctuary of The Beaconsfield Inn, sip a glass of sherry, and revel in the cultivated quiet.

Plum and Pineapple Chutney

Makes 4-5 pints

A sweet and sour combination, this chutney creates a fine appetizer served over cream cheese with sliced baguette served alongside. It would also be a good accompaniment to roast pork, grilled chicken or firm-fleshed fish.

20	red plums, pits removed and chopped
1	large pineapple, peeled, cored and chopped
2	large yellow onions, peeled and chopped
1	cup raisins
1	cup brown sugar
2	Tbs. chopped ginger root
1	tsp. allspice
1/2	tsp. coarsely ground pepper
1/2	tsp. dry mustard
1/2	tsp. nutmeg
1	Tbs. salt
1-1/4	cups cider vinegar

Place all ingredients except cider vinegar in a large saucepan over low heat. Cook, stirring, for 3-4 minutes, then add half the vinegar and simmer for 20 minutes, stirring occasionally.

Add remaining vinegar and continue to cook, gently, over low heat for about 1-1/2 hours, or until thick.

Prepare pint canning jars according to manufacturer instructions. Transfer chutney to jars, seal, cool, label and date.

Anyone who eats three meals a day
should understand why cookbooks outsell sex books
three to one.

L. M. Boyd

Heritage Harbour

1838 Ogden Avenue
Vancouver, B.C. V6J 1A1
Canada
Phone (604) 736-0809
Fax (604) 736-0074
Website: http://www.vancouver-bc.com/Heritage Harbour
Email: dhorner@direct.ca

Rates:
High Season: $155 Canadian
Low Season: $125 - 135 Canadian

Heritage Harbour

Heritage Harbour is a new house built with old-fashioned style. The three-storied home, painted a fetching shade of teal blue, features an array of window shapes and styles, accented with crisp, white paint, creating an eye-catching facade. Richard and Debra Horner built the house in 1993, the year they were married, and opened their doors as a bed and breakfast in 1996. Debra says the progression from home to b&b was quite natural. "We had family and friends visiting all the time, anyway. We're close to the city, and across the street from the beach, so our location couldn't be more ideal", she says. After years as a legal assistant, Debra was ready to shift gears into a new career, so the pieces fell together nicely. She researched the industry, experimented with recipes on family members and organized the second floor into two guest rooms and a lounge.

The airy, two-story entry hall is dominated by an enormous stained-glass window, custom-designed for the Horners by artist Yves Trudeau. The translucent silver, mauve and purple glass is highlighted with touches of blue and features components of the legendary phoenix and the centuries-old symbol of hospitality, the pineapple. Additional stained glass surrounds the front door and fills the frames of French doors dividing the living and dining rooms from the hallway, resulting in one of the largest collections of stained glass in Vancouver.

Debra sampled 52 colors on the living room and dining room walls before choosing deep teal for the formal living area with its classic fireplace and plum for the neighboring dining room. White wainscotting unites the two spaces, which are decorated with an attractive selection of Oriental rugs, and a mix of antique and contemporary furnishings.

More color saturates the walls in the guest lounge, a warm terra cotta-colored room with black leather sofas, oak wainscotting and a marble-faced gas fireplace. Large windows show off a spectacular view of English

Bay and the Vancouver skyline. Debra serves coffee and tea here, along with a freshly-baked treat, in the hour before breakfast each morning. A small fridge and self-serve beverages allow guests to stash snacks and

enjoy refreshments throughout the day. Those travelling on business or guests wishing to check their e-mail will appreciate the spare phone jack installed for laptops. There is also a computer available for guest use, along with a fax and photocopier.

The large second-floor hallway is lit by the glow of stained glass and ushers guests into Heritage Harbour's two rooms. The Harbour Room enjoys the same panoramic English Bay view as the guest lounge, with the added pleasure of French doors and a tiny terrace. The Garden Room also features French doors which lead to a large, sunny terrace, replete with patio furniture and flower boxes. Both rooms offer queen beds, antique furniture accents and good-sized private baths.

Heritage Harbour is located in the stylish westside neighborhood of Kitsilano Beach and sits conveniently between two parks, Vanier and Kitsilano. A short stroll brings guests to West 4th Avenue, home to the hip eateries and trendy shops for which the area is known. Guests can also walk waterfront trails to shop at the Granville Island Market, or head to Kits Beach to take a dip in the 120-metre heated outdoor swimming pool. Downtown Vancouver can be reached on foot, or hop on the pedestrian-only ferry and zip across False Creek for faster access.

Debra has lots of ideas for guests as well, and likes to spend time offering suggestions for where to go and what to do in the area. She'll dish out ideas while serving a healthy four-course breakfast. Guests can plan their day while savoring fresh fruit smoothies, homemade dried cranberry granola, scrambled eggs with smoked salmon and herbs or Dutch apple pancakes. Debra strives to serve tasty dishes that are relatively low in fat and cholesterol, always offering fresh fruit or smoothies, substituting turkey sausage for pork and using egg substitutes on occasion. Her love of baking ensures a steady supply of homemade Italian bread, a variety of quick breads and freshly baked cinnamon buns. Port and sherry are offered each afternoon between four and six o'clock for arriving guests and returning sightseers.

Cranberry Blueberry Raisin Bread

Yield: One 9 x 5 loaf or 4 mini loaves

Debra often substitutes the orange juice with fruit smoothie when making this bread.

2	cups flour
1	cup sugar
1-1/2	tsp. baking powder
1/2	tsp. baking soda
1/4	cup margarine
1	medium egg, or egg substitute
1	tsp. grated orange rind
1	tsp. grated lemon rind
3/4	cup freshly squeezed orange juice or fruit smoothie
1	cup raisins
1	cup blueberries, fresh or frozen
1	cup cranberries, fresh or frozen

Preheat oven to 350° F. Coat with vegetable spray one 9" x 5" x 3" loaf pan or four 5" x 3" x 2" mini loaf pans.

Sift together dry ingredients. Cut in margarine. In a separate bowl, mix egg or egg replacement with grated rinds, juice, raisins, blueberries and cranberries.

Add wet ingredients to dry ingredients and stir until just moistened. Transfer batter to loaf pan(s) and bake 70-75 minutes for single loaf or 35-40 minutes for mini loaves.

Cool in pan slightly and turn out onto rack to cool completely.

Freezes exceptionally well.

Laburnam Cottage

1388 Terrace Avenue North
Vancouver, B.C. V7R 1B4
Canada
Phone (604) 988-4877
Fax (604) 988-4877

Rates:
High Season: $145 - 225 Canadian
Low Season: $95 - 175 Canadian

Laburnum Cottage

Delphine Masterton had threatened to open her home as a bed and breakfast for years. It was something of a family joke until, in 1985, Delphine did just that. Raising five children and three decades in the travel industry provided her with ample experience to draw upon. A bumpy beginning was soon forgotten as waves of visitors to Expo '86 filled the house and spread the word of Delphine's hospitality. A steady stream of guests has continued since that time, enjoying the gracious ambiance and warm reception offered by Delphine, her family and assistant, Karen Essinger.

The charming cottage is surrounded by mature trees and blooming flowers. Planted by the first owner, the English-style garden has been lovingly tended by Delphine since she moved in 40 years ago and it annually receives a Garden of Excellence Award from a local gardening organization. The laburnum tree for which the cottage is named is tucked into the virgin woods at the edge of the property. The sunken horseshoe-shaped rose garden is an enchanting location for wedding ceremonies. Two small footbridges cross the little creek flowing through the garden, one of which leads to the Summer House, a fairy-tale bungalow popular with honeymooners. Guests are welcome to meander through the lush green beds or ponder the world from the covered porch.

Inside Laburnum Cottage, guests will find an elegant plum-walled drawing room handsomely decorated with antiques and interesting collectibles, including a lovely array of porcelains. Delphine knows the story of each piece, whether inherited from family or collected during her travels and has some intriguing history lessons to offer as a result.

More history is chronicled in the kitchen, where heirlooms decorate the open shelves and Beatrix Potter characters brighten the tiled walls. A large oak table in the center of the kitchen welcomes guests to be seated and another dining area is adjacent in the terra cotta-tiled breakfast room. The warm kitchen stars a massive AGA cooker, which provides heat and cooks up a mean pancake. Other tasty fare from the AGA include seafood- or vegetable-filled crepes, French toast, omelets, frittatas, coffee cakes and tender biscuits with homemade jams. Karen, Delphine's assistant, does the majority of cooking and guests will enjoy the camaraderie of Karen and Delphine in the kitchen while they dine. Just off the breakfast room is another small garden, where explorers will discover a tiny house, fully furnished, awaiting elfin residents.

Four guest rooms are located on the second floor of the cottage, each comfortable and well-appointed with a queen bed and private bath. The English Garden Room, on the ground floor, is a convenient option for families with a sleeping loft for the children, king bed for the adults, fireplace and kitchen facilities. Honeymooners won't be the only guests to enjoy the Summer House which contains a small kitchen, double bed, fireplace and private bath.

Laburnum Cottage's North Vancouver location feels extremely secluded, yet a fifteen-minute trip will have visitors downtown or at Horseshoe Bay. Just minutes away are the popular attractions of Grouse Mountain and the Capilano Suspension Bridge. At Grouse Mountain, tourists can ride up the mountain via aerial tramway to a spectacular view of the city skyline. The 450-foot long suspension bridge traverses a deep, tree-filled gorge, and the surrounding park is home to totem poles and an outdoor display depicting the story of the bridge. Whistler Mountain Resort, a world-class ski destination, is only 90 minutes from the cottage. Should guests prefer more sedate pastimes, there are walking trails nearby and Laburnum Cottage serves afternoon tea upon request.

Blueberry Coffee Cake

Serves 16

- 1/2 cup butter
- 1 cup sugar
- 3 eggs, beaten
- 1 tsp. baking powder
- 1 Tbs. baking soda
- 2 cups flour
- 1/4 tsp. salt
- 3/4 cup buttermilk
- 2 cups blueberries

Topping
- 1 cup brown sugar
- 1/4 cup butter
- 1/3 cup flour

Preheat oven to 375° F. Lightly grease 10" x 8" baking pan.

Beat together butter and sugar till fluffy. Add beaten eggs and mix well. Sift together dry ingredients and add to butter mixture alternately with buttermilk.

Fold in blueberries. Pour batter into prepared pan. Mix topping ingredients and spread evenly over batter.

Cover pan with foil and bake for 20 minutes. Remove foil and bake for another 15-20 minutes, or until golden brown.

Serve warm, topped with whipping cream if desired.

I do not think anything serious should be done after dinner,
as nothing should be done before breakfast.

George Saintsbury

The Old Farmhouse

1077 North End Road
Salt Spring Island, B.C. V8K 1L9
Canada
Phone (250) 537-4113
Fax (250) 537-4969
Website: http://www.pixsel.be.ca/bb/1182.htm
Email: farmhouse@saltspring.com

Rates:
High Season: $180 Canadian
Low Season: $150 Canadian

The Old Farmhouse

A four-hour stopover on Salt Spring Island changed Gerti and Karl Fusses' lives forever. In that brief span of time, a chance meeting with a realtor produced a perfect house whose potential as bed and breakfast Gerti saw immediately. After a brief negotiation, the Fusses returned home to Vancouver, proud owners of The Old Farmhouse, an 1894 homestead farm. The combination of the boat ride home and the enormity of their actions made Gertie become ill, but nine months later The Old Farmhouse bed and breakfast was born.

Gerti Fuss

Gerti and Karl live in the original farmhouse while guests stay in the guest wing designed by an architect to mirror the original building. The design was a success as many people ask which building is old and which is new. Gerti and Karl scoured antique stores as it was built, searching for windows, doors and hardware to keep the turn-of the century feel consistent from one building to another.

The guest wing has a private entrance and houses four spacious rooms offering either private balconies or patios. Feather beds and fluffy duvets, crisp white wainscotting and fresh flowers are just of few of the pleasant features in each room, along with the convenience of private baths. The attractive decor and comfortable surroundings have caused many a guest to comment on how the inn "looks like it's right out of the pages of House Beautiful," or that Gerti's hospitality was "just like visiting Grandma."

Gerti's hospitality begins first thing in the morning when she delivers coffee and tea to her guest's doors. After a cup or two, everyone heads to the main house for Gerti's famous breakfast. Guests won't find bacon and eggs or blueberry pancakes. "I like to prepare things people don't normally get at home," comments Gerti, "and I like to make it special by putting linen on the table and using fine china and silver." Staples at the table are cinnamon buns, croissants and muffins, baked fresh each morning. Island-grown berries are served with crème fraiche, also made by Gerti. Entrees range from soufflés to poached eggs on polenta with bearnaise sauce.

During the day, guests are free to wander the pleasant grounds or explore the island. Bring along a bike or rent one for touring rolling hills or spend an afternoon hiking and picnicking. Ply the waters surrounding the island on sailboat or fishing charters or paddle along the shoreline in a kayak. Salt Spring Island is well-known as an artist's colony and any number of galleries showcase the work of residents. The Saturday Farmer's Market is the place to find local produce and crafts from Easter through late September.

Returning to The Old Farmhouse, a nap in the hammock or curling up with a book in one of the outdoor nooks and crannies could wind down the day. Gerti and Karl are on hand to serve tea and offer guests suggestions for dinner – their favorites are House Piccolo for seafood, Hastings House for formal dining or Moby's for more casual, pub fare. The Fusses find that guests are quite convivial with one another, and often gather in the living room to visit. And though there is a television available, more often than not, it remains dark while new friends are made over a bottle of wine.

Vanilla Soufflé

Serves 2 as an entrée or 4 as dessert

Gerti notes, "If you have never made a soufflé before, this is the one to try. You will never be intimidated again. And it needs no collar."

1/2 cup milk	2 egg yolks
1 vanilla bean	2 egg whites
pinch salt	1-1/2 tsp. cornstarch
1 oz. butter	1 oz. sugar
1 oz. flour	

Preheat the oven to 375° F. Take a pan large enough to hold soufflé dishes and fill with 2-3 inches of water and place in oven while preheating. Prepare soufflé dishes by smearing inside with soft butter, then sprinkle with sugar.

With hands, mix the flour and butter to make a dough. Set aside.

In a saucepan, place the milk. Split the vanilla bean in half lengthwise and scrape out the mark, adding the mark and the bean to the milk and bring milk slowly to the boiling point.

Remove from heat and let it steep for a few minutes, adding the pinch of salt. Take the bean out of the milk, and scrape it clean between your fingers, so that any remaining marrow is in the milk. Put the milk back on the heat and with a wire whisk, add bit by bit the butter-flour mixture. It will resemble a big lump. Now add the egg yolks, one at a time, and incorporate well with whisk. (At this point you may add 3T. of Grand Marnier or 3 T. of best-quality melted chocolate for an orange or chocolate soufflé.)

In a large bowl, beat the egg whites with the cornstarch and the sugar to a stiff peak. Take about 2 tablespoonfuls of egg white and incorporate into the soufflé batter. Using a wire whisk, carefully fold in remaining egg white and scoop into soufflé dishes.

Place soufflé dishes in water bath in oven and bake for 15 minutes, or 12 minutes if preparing 4 portions. Remove from oven, sprinkle with powdered sugar and serve at once.

Cheese Blintzes with Blueberry Sauce

Makes 15-18 blintzes

Crêpe Batter
- 1 cup flour
- 1/3 cup sugar
- 1/2 cup melted butter
- grated rind of an orange
- pinch salt
- 2-1/2 cups milk
- 5 eggs
- 1/2 cup melted butter, plus additional for making the crêpes

Crêpe Filling
- 1 cup cream cheese
- 1 cup Quark or small curd cottage cheese
- grated rind of a lemon
- pinch salt
- 1/2 cup sugar

Blueberry Sauce
- 2 cups fresh or frozen blueberries
- 1/2 cup sugar
- 1 Tbs. cornstarch
- 1/2 cup water

For the crêpes: In a medium bowl, combine the flour, sugar, salt, eggs and the orange rind. Add the milk, plus the butter and with a wire whisk or and electric mixer beat the batter until no lumps remain. Set aside for 2 hours.

For the filling: Combine all ingredients in a food processor, and pulse for 10 seconds, scrape down the sides with a rubber spatula and blend for another 20 seconds or until smooth or blend ingredients in a medium bowl with an electric mixer until smooth. Set aside.

Continued on next page

Blueberry Sauce

In a large saucepan, bring the blueberries and sugar to a gentle boil. In a small bowl, whisk together the water and cornstarch and stir into the boiling fruit. As soon as the sauce thickens, remove and set aside or refrigerate for later use.

To make the Blintzes: Heat an 8-10" crêpe or omelet pan over medium high heat and brush with melted butter. Pour in 3-4 tablespoons of batter, immediately tilting the pan in all directions and swirling the batter so it covers the bottom of the pan in a very thin layer.

Return to heat and cook until the bottom is slightly browned, turn with a spatula and brown the other side for a few seconds.

Slide the crêpe on a flat surface and place about 1 tablespoon of the filling down the center of the crêpe. Fold about 1/2 inch of crêpe at the bottom and top over filling and then fold each side over filling. If serving immediately, set aside and keep warm until ready to use, or if freezing for later use, place filled crêpes on a cookie sheet and place in freezer for one hour until firm. Then wrap in foil and return to freezer for later use.

To serve, spoon 2 tablespoons for blueberry sauce onto center of plate and place 2 blintzes on top of sauce. Sprinkle with powdered sugar and garnish with fresh blueberries, and serve at once.

If serving frozen blintzes, remove from freezer and bake at 350° F until warmed through, about 20 minutes.

Making love without love is like
trying to make a soufflé without egg whites.

Simone Beck

Penny Farthing Inn

2855 West 6th Avenue
Vancouver, B.C. V6K 1X2
Canada
Phone (604) 739-9002
Fax (604) 739-9004
Website: http://www.vancouver-bc.com/PennyFarthing
Email: farthing@uniserve.com

Rates:
High Season: $95 - 165 Canadian
Low Season: $75 - 140 Canadian

Penny Farthing Inn

The Penny Farthing Inn is a cheerful blue Heritage House, built in 1912, located on a quiet side street in the fashionable Kitsilano neighborhood. The hustle and bustle of trendy West Fourth Avenue seems far away as visitors arrive, greeted by a colorful garden and friendly cats. The impression deepens as visitors climb the stairs to the old-fashioned wicker-filled porch, and enter the inn. Dark wood trim, hardwood floors, stained glass windows and antique furniture usher guests back in time. The Penny Farthing was named for an 1870s bicycle whose large front wheel (an old penny) was paired with a small rear wheel (a farthing – a quarter of an old penny).

Two suites and two rooms have appropriately old-fashioned names; Abigail, Bettina, Sophie and Lucinda. Abigail commands the top floor of the Penny Farthing, tucked beneath the eaves and lit by a large skylight. The bedroom overlooks the front garden while the sitting area enjoys a mountain and skyline view. Additional amenities include a sofa bed, private bath and TV/VCR. Bettina offers a porch with partial view, sitting room with television and VCR, and pine four-poster bed in addition to a private bath. Sophie and Lucinda share a bathroom, with Sophie sporting another pine four-poster while Lucinda has the option of two twin or one king bed. All rooms have telephones and mini refrigerators, and guests have access to a fax machine and e-mail.

Videophiles will be especially pleased by the collection of 120+ films available for their enjoyment. A television and VCR are located in the lounge on the first floor. Guests can relax here enjoying a movie, reading or enjoying a CD or two. Perhaps one of the resident felines will curl up alongside for cat nap.

Guests eat well while staying at Penny Farthing. Innkeeper Lyn Hainstock prepares what she calls, "just delicious food, attractively presented." Strawberry crêpes, apple and brie frittatas or eggs benedict might be the main attraction, but equally compelling are freshly baked scones, croissants and muffins, served with homemade jams and jellies. Exotic fruits such as mango and papaya are served with fresh berries and melons. Winter will find guests dining cozily in the dark wood-paneled dining room. In summer, breakfast is served on  the brick patio, amid the blooms of the perennial garden and the scent of herbs. Lyn offers a pick-me-up of appetizers and sherry in the late afternoon.

Good food abounds in the Kits Beach neighborhood. The Penny Farthing is surrounded by small ethnic cafes, offering visitors a chance to sample cuisines from the world over – Ethiopian, East Indian, Italian, Thai, Szechuan – and local fare featuring exquisite seafood. The student population at nearby University of British Columbia ensures a wealth of coffee bars and espresso hang-outs for caffeine needy visitors.

The Penny Farthing's location offers more than a great variety of food and drink. Convenient access to downtown Vancouver, Kitsilano Beach, and the University offer plenty of attractions and a steady stream of festivals occupies the summer months, from music to film to fireworks.

Dutch Butter Cake

    2/3   cup butter
      1   cup sugar
    1-1/2 tsp. almond extract
      1   egg, beaten (reserve 2t. for glazing cake)
    1-1/2 cups flour
    1/2   tsp. baking powder
    1/2   cup whole almonds, skinned and blanched

Continued on next page

Preheat oven to 350° F. Lightly grease 8" square pan or 9" pie tin.

Beat together butter, sugar and almond extract until well blended. Add beaten egg, reserving 2 tsp. for glaze.

Sift together flour and baking powder and add to butter mixture, combining well. Press batter evenly into prepared pan and brush with remaining egg. Decorate top with almonds. Bake for 30 minutes or until light golden brown. Cut into wedges to serve.

Scones

Makes 12-14

This basic scone recipe can be made as is, or add one of the suggested "extras" for variation.

- 2 cups flour
- 1/2 tsp. salt
- 4 tsp. baking powder
- 1/4 cup butter
- 1 cup buttermilk

Preheat oven to 400° F. Place all ingredients except buttermilk into work bowl of a food processor and blend well. Add buttermilk and blend until it combines into a tube rising from the bottom to the top of the bowl.

Turn out onto floured surface and add EXTRAS (see below) Knead 10-15 times until smooth and well mixed. Roll out to approximately 1/2" thick and cut out with a 2" cookie cutter or form into a round and cut into 6-8 wedges.

Place 1/2" apart on a baking sheet and bake for 10-12 minutes, or until golden. Serve with butter and homemade jams and jellies.

EXTRAS: raisins • blueberries • cranberries with grated orange zest chopped dried apricots • diced candied ginger • grated cheese with herbs • chopped strawberries with grated lemon zest or orange zest

Richview House

7031 Richview Drive, R. R. 4
Sooke, B.C. V0S 1N0
Canada
Phone (250) 642-5520
Fax (250) 739-9004
Website: http://www.islandnet.com/~rvh
Email: rvh@islandnet.com

Rates: $145 - 195 Canadian

Richview House

Sooke is named for the local T'Souke Indian tribe, whose ancestors arrived, according to legend, in a copper box, which fell from heaven to earth. Contemporary arrivals likely have reached Sooke more ordinarily, but the natural beauty of the area inclines some to think the T'Souke's predecessors brought a bit of heaven with them when they landed.

The peace and serenity found in Sooke is echoed at Richview House. François and Joan Gething have created their own version of heaven at their bed and breakfast inn. Set atop an 80-foot cliff, Richview House commands an unobstructed panorama of the Strait of Juan de Fuca and the Olympic Mountains in the distance. Eagles soar overhead while otters and sea lions frolic below.

The original home, resembling a Norman farmhouse, was built by François' parents in 1967. The inn portion was added in 1991, by Francois, who also acted as designer, finish carpenter and furniture-builder. The interior is warmed by Douglas fir floors and yellow cedar trim. Simplicity and craftsmanship are the hallmarks of this restful residence.

There are but three rooms at Richview House, lending a distinct air of privacy to the inn. Two rooms upstairs are mirror images, down to the in-room fireplace and swirling jacuzzi on the deck. The downstairs room is appointed with a hand-crafted suite of furniture made by François from a single alder log. The double-headed shower becomes a steam bath with the twist of a handle. An array of herbal oils is available to create a private aromatherapy session while in the shower. All of the rooms are decorated with works from local and Northwest artists.

Collect a walking stick from the mud room and venture outside. A broad lawn stretches from the house to cliff's edge, home to climbing roses, flowering perennials, bright shrubs and thick hedges. Cedar benches, weathered silver gray, are placed in sun and shade for viewing the gardens and Strait.

The mild climate is but one attraction to the area. Sooke's natural harbor is haven to many boats and the Strait of Juan de Fuca home to many fish. Ancient cedar and hemlock forests have created a booming logging industry as well as sheltering numerous hiking trails. The sea is a draw to sport fisherman, kayakers and whale watchers. Mountain bikers and hikers will enjoy East Sooke Regional Park with trails timed from thirty minutes to six hours. Naturalists and driftwood collectors can stroll along Whiffen Spit, a natural breakwater protecting the harbor from the Strait, to view native plants and pick up a souvenir or two. Those interested in natural history should visit the Sooke Regional Museum to learn more about the history and economy of the region.

Sooke's benevolent weather is a boon to many gardeners. Joan Gething has created lovely gardens on the grounds at Richview House, as well as a vegetable garden that supplies both family and guests. Organic farmers on the island are another source of diverse produce. Blackberries grow in profusion, providing fruit for jam and sauces. Strawberries and raspberries grow well too, along with more unusual varieties like tayberries and loganberries.

Menus are inspired by the variety of local ingredients. One favorite is corn meal waffles, made from corn Joan grows and cracks herself. The waffles are served with maple syrup and sautéd apples. The Gethings smoke their own salmon and it turns up tucked into crêpes, sauced with maple yogurt. Crêpes are also filled with a range of fruits, depending on the season, and topped with an orange ginger sauce. Fruit selections might include cantaloupe topped with ginger and mint or papaya drizzled with cinnamon syrup. Joan makes her own French bread, to enjoy with sweet butter and homemade jams. Guests gather in the dining room for breakfast or Joan will provide room service upon request.

Tell me what you eat
and I will tell you what you are.

Brillat-Savarin

I wonder if Brillat-Savarin's grand bluff
was ever called?

Jay Jacobs
Gourmet

Fruit Crêpes with French Vanilla Yogurt and Orange Ginger Sauce

Serves 4

The crêpe batter and sauce can be made in advance. In the morning, prepare fruit filling and reheat sauce while making crêpes.

Crêpes

- 3/4 cup milk
- 2 eggs
- 1/2 cup flour
- 1 Tbs. melted butter

Mix all ingredients together well. Refrigerate overnight.

To make crêpes, heat a lightly oiled 10" skillet over medium heat. Pour 1/4 cup batter into skillet, lifting and tilting skillet to spread batter evenly over entire surface. Return skillet to heat, cooking crêpe until golden, turn crêpe with a spatula and brown the other side for a few seconds.

Invert pan over paper towel-lined plate and continue making crêpes until all batter is used.

Fruit Filling

- 1 medium apple, peeled, cored and sliced
- 2 Tbs. butter
- 2 cups blueberries
- 1/4 cup raspberries
- 1/2 cup pitted cherries

Melt butter in a medium saucepan over medium heat. Add apples and saute gently. Add remaining fruit and heat through. Set aside until ready to use.

Continued on next page

Orange-Ginger Sauce

    2 Tbs. grated fresh ginger
    1 Tbs. grated orange rind
    1/2 cup orange juice
    1/2 cup water
    1 cup sugar
    2 Tbs. corn syrup

Combine all ingredients in saucepan and bring to a boil over medium heat and boil for 5 minutes. Will keep, covered, in refrigerator.

Assembling the Crêpes

    Crêpes
    Fruit Filling
    Orange-Ginger Sauce
    8 oz. French Vanilla Yogurt
    Blueberries and raspberries, optional

Place one crêpe on each plate. Spoon 1/4 of fruit sauce in center of crêpe and top with two tablespoons of yogurt. Fold sides of crêpe over filling and drizzle with one tablespoon orange-ginger sauce. Dust plate rim with powdered sugar and garnish with additional berries if desired.

And every day when I've been good,
I get an orange after food.

Robert Louis Stevenson

Sooke Harbour House

1528 Whiffen Spit Road
Sooke, B.C., V0S 1N0
Canada
Phone (250) 642-3421
Toll Free (800) 889-9688
Fax (250) 642-6988
Web Site: http://www.sookenet.com/sooke/shh
Email: shh@islandnet.com

High Season: $270 - 465 Canadian
Low Season: $200 - 340 Canadian

Sooke Harbour House

Wild cuisine is the latest trend to catch the attention of foodies nationwide. Savvy restauranteurs are wowing patrons with novel ingredients, foraged from sea, forest and field. This is regional cuisine on an introspective basis, focusing on ingredients growing, literally, just outside the back door.

The Pacific Northwest's back door opens onto the granddaddy of wild cuisine, Sooke Harbour House. The passionate creation of Sinclair and Fredrica Philip, whose vision of serving seasonal, organic regional foods has made the inn world-renowned for both the quality and originality of its fare and accommodations. The Philips came to Sooke in 1979, when this kind of dedication to local products was almost unknown in North America.

All menu ingredients, with precious few exceptions, come from the inn's gardens and farm or from nearby producers practicing organic farming methods. At Sooke Harbour House regional translates to extremely local – far away means 30 miles in regards to foodstuffs, a characteristic perhaps rarer now, in our increasingly global economy, than two decades ago when the Philips opened their doors to a curious public.

Over the years, the Philips have worked with ethnobotantist, Dr. Nancy Turner, to develop native plant materials for use in the restaurant. Dr. Turner is a specialist in the foods of the First Nation, native residents of Vancouver Island. As a result, camas bulb, licorice fern root, miner's lettuce, Coast Salish nodding onion, cow's parsnip, chickweed, Indian celery, Oregon grape, salal berries and wild gooseberries are regular players in the ever-changing theatre of the dining room.

BED & BREAKFAST INNS OF BRITISH COLUMBIA

Many Northwest restaurants serving fish and shellfish have a fresh tank to hold their catch. Sooke Harbour House has the Strait of Juan de Fuca. Sinclair and others don wet suits and tanks to dive into the chilly waters below the inn to gather the next meal's inspiration. This fresh tank par excellence offers up the rare and unusual on a daily basis; goosenecked barnacles, limpets, abalone, purple-hinged rock scallops, giant acorn barnacles, geoduck, and sea cucumber. Local fisherman bring rockfish, wolffish, cabezon and sculpin, caught in nearby Port Renfrew or Sooke proper. The vagaries of Mother Nature don't allow for advance planning - menus are designed just hours before serving, dependent upon the day's catch.

Twenty to thirty different flowers and greens compose a salad. The mild climate allows a twelve-month growing season, ensuring guests in December food as fresh and interesting as one might expect in July. Terraced beds surround the inn and the beauty of the gardens belies their intrinsic purpose as larder. The kaleidoscopic array is maintained by six full-time gardeners tending to over 400 varieties of plants, flowers, herbs and edible weeds, all fodder for the imaginative team in the kitchen. If following Sinclair on a tour, be prepared for a whirlwind education. Plant names are tossed off quickly; walking stick cabbage, wild sorrel, garlic chives, sweet woodruff, oxeye daisy. Leaves plucked, then crushed, for a whiff of pineapple sage or taste of Vietnamese coriander. Explanations offered – just how does one use begonia and nasturtium tubers in cooking?

Of course, the very best way to see how all of these pieces become one on the dinner plate is to spend an evening in the warm and casually elegant dining room. White linen-covered tables are scattered across two rooms, simply dressed with tapers and a flower. The Strait of Juan de Fuca sparkles outside and the massive peaks of the Olympic Mountains loom in the distance. The quixotic menu is hand-written; the chance of eating the same thing twice essentially non-existent.

An introduction to the local flora can be had by ordering the Sooke Harbour House salad. To meet the fauna, select leg of Matchosin rabbit or slow-roasted rack of veal from nearby Cedar Glen Farm. Seafood is the specialty of the house and offerings range from a simple dungeness crab, served whole with nodding onion butter to the more complex; consomme of red rock crab, garnished with sea cucumber and brined herring roe on red laver seaweed and Indian celery umbels or Chinook salmon with a Grand Fir-infused fireweed honey, enrobed in sea lettuce with evergreen huckleberry, sweet cicely and hazelnut sauce. The wine list offers an extensive selection of varietals from British Columbia, perhaps the ideal libation to accompany Sooke's fare. Those wishing to imbibe grapes from farther afield shan't be disappointed – the vineyards of California, Washington, France and Germany are represented, too.

Finish the meal with a delectable sweet; lemon verbena infused apricot sorbet, strawberries in sweet cicely sabayon, millefeuille of caramelized orange cox pippin apples or Sooke garden figs poached in red wine. The wonderful late harvest and ice wines of B.C. would be just the ticket to close the evening, sipped while seated on the sofa facing the river rock fireplace.

The allure of a crackling fire can be enjoyed in each of the guest suites as well. Ensconsed in comfort, enjoy a glass of port, thoughtfully provided by the hosts. A recent remodel, connecting the 1928 inn and a later, freestanding addition, has doubled the original number of rooms. The transition is seamless, and Fredrica's exquisite taste and elegance is echoed throughout in the interior design. The caliber of accommodations is equal to the level of skill in the dining room. Each room is unique, a composition of carefully selected furnishings and accessories designed to delight and surprise. One favorite is the Victor Newman Longhouse Room, a showcase for the Kwaikutl artist's masks and paddles. A carved chiefs chair dominates one corner.

BED & BREAKFAST INNS OF BRITISH COLUMBIA

The Driftwood Room, in the newly added wing, sports a "bouch" – a boat made into a couch. A slab of golden wood supported by six knobby legs forms a bench doing double duty as coffee table. The bathroom's enormous mirror is framed in more driftwood, collected on strolls along Whiffen Spit. Additional thematic treatments highlight the natural world outside Sooke Harbour House and feature hummingbirds, fish and an underwater orchard, to name but a few.

Relax in a soothing jetted tub, another luxury touch. Some tubs are inside, some outside and several rooms sport both! Flowers boxes grace the decks of upstairs rooms, and below, private terraces have rosemary hedges or evergreen clematis trellises to screen them. Cushioned chaise lounges beckon for a sunbath while admiring the spectral view.

When guests awake, breakfast is delivered to their door. Coffee beans and oranges don't grow on Vancouver Island, but fear not. These morning staples are an exception to the rule of local products. Herbs, however, grow profusely, and are used for a wide variety of teas. Salmon-stuffed rosemary bread, maple walnut muffins, lavender popovers with honey sauce and hazelnut-maple syrup waffles are just a few of the enticements to getting out of bed.

There truly is no need to leave Sooke Harbour House once visitors arrive. The tariff includes breakfast as well as lunch, which is served buffet-style in the dining room or request a picnic basket, replete with china and flatware. Dinner awaits, at the end of the day, in one of the best dining rooms in Canada. While there is plenty to do in Sooke, perhaps the very best thing to do is nothing at all.

Dutch Baby Pancake with Red Huckleberry-Maple Syrup Puree

Serves 2

Dutch babies traditionally are baked in iron skillets. Two 6" skillets are needed to prepare this recipe for individual servings. One 12" skillet, pie pans or cake pans can be substituted.

- 3 large eggs
- 1/2 cup flour
- 1/2 cup milk
- pinch sea salt
- 4 Tbs. unsalted butter
- pinch nutmeg (optional)

Preheat oven to 450° F.

In a one quart bowl, lightly whisk the eggs for 15 seconds.

Add the flour, whisking until the mixture is quite smooth, about 1 minute. Add milk, and whisk until batter is uniform in texture. Blend in sea salt and nutmeg, if desired. Strain the mixture through a coarse strainer to remove any lumps. Discard lumps and set batter aside.

Heat the two cast iron skillets over medium heat on top of the stove. Melt 2 T. butter in each pan. When butter is melted, pour half the batter into each pan.

Immediately remove the pans from the top of stove and place in the preheated oven for approximately 10-12 minutes, or until the raised pancake is golden in color.

During the last 2 minutes of baking, place two dinner plates in the oven. Remove the dutch babies from the oven and transfer to the warmed plates and serve immediately.

Red or Black Huckleberry-Maple Syrup Puree

2	cups black Evergreen huckleberries or red huckleberries
1	cup pear cider
1/4	cup maple syrup
	additional maple syrup for drizzling over Dutch baby

Put berries and cider in medium saucepan over medium heat. Bring slowly to simmer and simmer for 10 minutes. Remove from heat and cool slightly.

Transfer berry and cider mixture to a blender or food processor. Add the maple syrup and puree for about 1 minute.

Pour puree into Dutch Baby. If desired, drizzle a small amount of maple syrup over the top. Garnish with fresh black or red huckleberries and fresh blackberries.

Give me the luxuries of life
and I will gladly live without the necessities.

Frank Lloyd Wright

Oyster Bars

Serves 4

Hazelnut flour dusted oysters are layered between crispy potatoes and wild greens, then drizzled with vinaigrette created from organic hazelnut oil, fresh horseradish and garlic chives. Don't let the length of the recipe intimidate you – it's actually quite easy to prepare.

Vinaigrette

- 1/2 tsp. freshly grated horseradish
- 2 Tbs. organic, cold-pressed hazelnut oil
- 2 Tbs. organic, cold-pressed canola oil
- 2 Tbs. organic apple cider vinegar
- 1/2 tsp. Dijon mustard
- 1-1/2 tsp. boiling water
- 1 tsp. chopped garlic chives (regular chives can be substituted, if necessary)

In a small bowl or food processor, whisk together all ingredients except the boiling water and chives. When the mixture is emulsified, continue to whisk and add boiling water. Stir in the chives and set aside.

Crispy Potatoes

- 2 large Yukon Gold potatoes, peeled (russets can be substituted)
- 3 Tbs. unsalted butter, melted
- salt and pepper to taste
- parchment paper

Preheat oven to 450° F. Line a baking sheet with parchment paper.

Trim potatoes into blocks, 2" x 3", then cut potatoes into 1/8" thick slices. This should result in 12 potato slices, 2" x 3" x 1/8".

Brush half the melted butter on the parchment paper. Then lay the potato slices on the baking sheet and brush them with remaining butter. Season with salt and pepper to taste.

Cover with another sheet of parchment and bake for approximately 15 minutes, or until crispy. Keep warm until ready to use.

Wilted Bitter Greens

- 1 lb. assorted greens, trimmed and cleaned, such as mizuna, mustard, tat soi, kale, arugula, lamb's quarters or other stongly flavored greens
- 2 shallots, peeled and finely diced
- 2 Tbs. unsalted butter
- salt and pepper to taste

Heat the butter in a non-reactive (do not use aluminum or copper) skillet over medium heat until it starts to brown slightly.

Add shallots and cook for 30 seconds, then add the mixed greens. Season to taste with salt and pepper and toss until just wilted, about 20-30 seconds and set aside.

Pan-Fried Hazelnut Flour-Dusted Clayquot Oysters

- 16 large Clayquot Sound Pacific oysters (best if shucked just prior to preparation)
- 3 Tbs. hazelnut flour *
- 2 Tbs. unsalted butter

Dust the oysters with the hazelnut flour, shaking off any excess.

Heat the butter in a large frying pan over medium high heat until hot. Add the oysters and fry for about 1 to 2 minutes (depending upon their size) until golden. Set aside.

* If hazelnut flour is not available, grind toasted, skinned hazelnuts to a fine powder.

Assembly

    4   large dinner plates
        garlic chive flowers

Place one potato slice on each plate and cover with a thin layer of wilted greens. Top with 2 oysters and repeat process. Top each bar with remaining potato slice. Drizzle 1/4 of the vinaigrette over the top and around sides of each bar. Garnish with garlic chive flowers.

Oysters are the usual opening to a winter breakfast –
indeed, they are almost indispensable.

Almanach des Gourmands, 1803

Thistledown House

3910 Capilano Road
North Vancouver, B.C. V7R 4J2
Canada
Phone (604) 986-7173
Fax (604) 980-2939
Web Site: http://www.thistle-down.com
Email: davidson@helix.net

Rates: $110 - 189 Canadian

Thistledown House

The thistle is a well-recognized symbol of Scotland, but few know that many varieties of thistles also grow in Switzerland. When thinking of a name for their bed and breakfast inn, Canadian-born Scot Rex Davidson and Swiss-born Ruth Crameri were trying to find a common denominator, and came up with the thistle. But how to make it less prickly-sounding? Tossing the name around for a few days, Rex remembered a poem from his childhood that described snow, "falling as softly as thistledown". The gentle sentiment was deemed appropriate and a jar of the fluffy white thistledown now resides in the entry of Thistledown House.

Ruth and Rex came to innkeeping from hospitality backgrounds. Though Ruth is a practicing architect and interior designer, six generations of her family operated a small hotel in Switzerland, and Ruth spent summers tagging along with her mother when she helped her parents at their inn, exposing Ruth to many aspects of the profession. Rex, a journalist by trade, has been involved in variety of careers including owning and operating a five-star restaurant. The duo are extremely gracious, welcoming and hospitable, and truly enjoy their latest career. Ruth says that the inn often feels like "one big house party", with people laughing and having a wonderful time.

Thistledown wasn't originally intended to be an inn. Ruth and Rex bought it for their home, but realized that it had great potential as a bed and breakfast. Speeding up their "retirement" plans by a decade, Ruth resigned her position with a large architectural firm, and Rex began working from home. The business began with three rooms in the main house, and then, in the spring of '97, the inn closed for three months for remodeling. Ruth designed the addition, and found great pleasure in being her own client.

The result of the remodel is a seamless transition from old to new. The 1920 Craftsman features of the original home continue in the Wintergarden, a bright, sunny room overlooking the grounds at the rear of the house and the two new guest rooms. All of the guest rooms have a unique personality and are furnished with antique and hand-crafted treasures collected by Ruth and Rex. The luxurious Under the Apple Tree suite has a sunken sitting room with fireplace, king-size bed, private bath with jetted tub-for-two and a private patio for sunbathing. A private balcony is available to guests of Mulberry Peak, along with queen bed and private bath. Sweet Tibby is decorated with antique pine pieces and a handsome sleigh bed. A reading nook built for two and private bath with stained glass windows complete the room. Memories has a European flavor and the option of a king or two twin beds while the queen-bedded Snuggery is decorated with Persian carpets, rich colors and stained glass. Guests of both rooms enjoy private baths and all rooms offer cozy robes and fluffly down- or silk-filled duvets.

Guests are welcome to lounge fireside in the living room, or soak up the sun in the Wintergarden or on the outdoor deck. The Office is available to those needing to fax, e-mail, print or copy. Rex has a large collection of books on Scotland and his heritage and is delighted to share his knowledge. Plenty of books and magazines provide for a serious or casual read for all. Ruth and Rex like to sit down with their guests, maps and felt markers at hand, and help guide them to interesting destinations.

The inn is located in North Vancouver, and Ruth loves the location because, "the wilderness is five minutes one way and a cosmopolitan city is fifteen minutes the other way." The Capilano Suspension Bridge and 20

THE GOURMET'S GUIDE TO NORTHWEST BED & BREAKFAST INNS

miles of hiking trails are just across the street. Ruth and Rex have collected the menus of their favorite restaurants into a book available to guests. Check out Earl's just down the street for great Margaritas and a high-energy environment or CinCin for upscale Italian in Vancouver.

Food is a great attraction at Thistledown as well. In addition to a lavish breakfast, tea is served each afternoon. Ruth begins meals with a cereal course, offering genuine Swiss Bircher-meusli or Thistledown granola, followed by an array of freshly baked breads with sweet butter, European cranberry jam, Scottish marmalade and thistle honey. A fruit course is next, perhaps limed papaya, poached figs or grapefruit with sherried plum sauce. Main courses alternate between sweet and savory, perhaps chocolate waffles with bing cherry sauce one day and portobello mushrooms with ham in demiglace cream over four cheese polenta the next. In the late afternoon, melt-in-the-mouth butter cookies, freshly baked fruit tarts and chocolates accompany tea and coffee in the attractive Craftsman dining room.

———⋄———

So in our pride we ordered for breakfast an omelet,
toast and coffee and what has just arrived
is a tomato salad with onions, a dish of pickles,
a big slice of watermelon
and two bottles of cream soda.

John Steinbeck
Travelling in Russia

ThistleDown House Birchermuesli

Serves 6

Muesli is a German-Swiss word for "mush." Dr. Bircher-Brenner invented this combination of fruit, oats, nuts and dairy in 1895 to treat rickets-stricken children. Their rapid recovery proved his tasty recipe nutritionally sound and it has remained popular ever since.

- 2-1/2 cups old-fashioned rolled oats
- 1-1/2 cups water
- 1/4 cup honey
- zest of one lemon
- 1/2 cup lemon juice (3-4 lemons)
- 1/3 cup sugar
- 1/2 cup grated and flaked almonds, hazelnuts and seeds (pumpkin, sunflower, etc.)
- 2 cups fresh fruit (apples, oranges, bananas, berries, apricots, peaches, etc.)
- 2 cups whipped cream

Boil the water, add honey and stir to dissolve. Add lemon juice and zest. Put oats in heatproof glass bowl and pour liquid over. Let soak for a minimum of 2 hours or soak overnight.

Shortly before serving, add the nuts, seeds, fruit (cubed to bite-size). If using apples or bananas, stir in right away to avoid browning. Add sugar and honey to taste. The whole mixture should be nice and moist. Depending on the moisture content, add a bit of freshly-squeezed orange juice.

Fold in whipped cream. Serve immediately, maybe with a great chunk of homemade crusty bread.

Option: use plain yogurt instead of whipped cream. Do not use regular milk as it will curdle!

Refrigerate any leftovers, they make great snacks.

Chocolate Waffles with Bing Cherry Sauce

Serves 4

This dish is offered at ThistleDown only when fresh bing cherries are available.

Cherry Sauce

- 1/2 cup sugar
- 3/4 cup water
- 1 Tbs. Kirsch or cherry liqueur
- 1-1/2 cups fresh Bing cherries, pitted and halved
- 2 Tbs. cornstarch

In a medium saucepan, bring to a boil water and sugar. Add Kirsch or cherry liqueur and cherries. Return to boil.

Dissolve cornstarch in a little water, whisking to combine well. Add to cherry mixture and boil, stirring constantly until sauce has thickened.

Cover cherry sauce to keep warm and set aside.

Chocolate Waffles

- 1/2 cup salted butter at room temperature, plus additional melted butter for waffle iron
- 4 egg yolks
- 4 egg whites
- 1 tsp. baking soda
- 1-2/3 cups all-purpose flour
- 1-1/2 cups heavy cream
- 1/2 cup miniature chocolate chips

Heat waffle iron, thoroughly brushing iron plates with melted butter.

In a large bowl, beat egg whites until they form stiff peaks. Add baking soda and continue beating a few more seconds. In a medium bowl, beat together butter and egg yolks until frothy.

Alternating between the flour, heavy cream, chocolate chips and beaten egg whites, gently fold into the butter egg mixture until the batter is smooth and even.

Pour batter into the preheated iron and bake until golden brown. Serve immediately topped with cherry sauce and a dollop of whipped cream.

Rhubarb Pie

Makes one 10-inch pie

Whipped cream tastes wonderful with this slightly tart specialty Ruth's grandmother served decades ago in Switzerland.

Pastry

- 2 cups flour
- 1 tsp. salt
- 10 Tbs. unsalted butter
- 2 chilled egg yolks
- 2 Tbs. sugar
- 3-1/2 to 4 Tbs. cold water

In a large bowl, combine flour and salt. Using a pastry cutter or two knives, cut in butter until butter is the size of small peas.

Add egg yolks and sugar and mix with hands to combine well. Add cold water and mix until all is moistened. Chill pastry for 30 minutes.

Preheat oven to 375° F.

Roll out pastry to approximately 14" diameter and place in a straight-sided spring form pan, allowing pastry edges to drape over the top rim. Pierce bottom of crust several times with a fork.

Continued on next page

Spread evenly over pastry base:
- 1/2 cup bread crumbs
- 1/2 cup slivered almonds

And top with:
- 3 cups rhubarb, chopped into 1/4" pieces

Loosely roll pastry edges inward over rhubarb and glaze with a mixture of 1 egg yolk mixed with 1/2 tsp. sugar.

Bake for 20 minutes in the lower third of oven, then add filling:
- 2 eggs
- 1 egg yolk
- 1 cup heavy cream
- 4 Tbs. cornstarch
- 3/4 cup sugar
- 2 egg whites

Beat together eggs, egg yolk, heavy cream, cornstarch and sugar.

In a separate bowl, beat egg whites until soft peaks form, then fold into above mixture.

Pour filling over rhubarb and bake for an additional 45 minutes.

Allow to cool to room temperature and sprinkle with coarse sugar before serving.

A good laugh is sunshine in the house.

Wm. Makepeace Thackeray

Wilp Gybuu

Box 396, 311 Leighton Way
Tofino, B.C. V0R 2Z0
Canada
Phone (250) 725-2330
Fax (250) 725-1205
Web Site: http://www.vancouverisland-bc.com/
WilpGybuuBB
Email: wilpgybu@island.net

High Season: $80 - 90 Canadian
Low Season: $75 - 85 Canadian

Wilp Gybuu

Tofino, British Columbia, has an eclectic population. Old fisher families, ex-hippies, Vietnam War draft dodgers, artists and urban refugees co-exist in this small village of 1,200, located on the west coast of Vancouver Island. And while it is home to few, Tofino is a destination for one million visitors each year. Eco-tourism has arrived in Tofino and the areas' pristine environment draws people from around the world to walk unsullied beaches, whale watch, fish, kayak and hike through rainforests.

Wendy and Ralph Burgess host some of these tourists at their bed and breakfast, Wilp Gybuu (Wolf House in Native Gitksan). Wendy and Ralph had come to Tofino as tourists themselves, and were seeking a lifestyle change when the idea of operating a bed and breakfast came to them. Leaving their jobs in Vancouver, the Burgesses relocated to Tofino in 1991. Ralph is Native Gitksan, and creates gold and silver jewelry inspired by his heritage, while Wendy operates the inn.

Wendy spends a lot of time interacting with her guests and getting them acquainted with the unique features of Tofino and its surroundings. Suggestions are made for outdoor activities, spots to dine, galleries to browse and stores to shop. Settled in one of three rooms, guests can enjoy the serene decor which reflects the name of each; the Salal, home to a queen bed and gas fireplace; the Cedar, also with a queen bed; and the twin-bed furnished Alder, home to another gas fireplace. First Nations, west coast and contemporary art add to the sense of place in each room.

The guest lounge sports a pair of well-cushioned sofas to encourage relaxation. A television is available, should anyone wish to check on the outside world, and those with musical inclinations can tickle the ivories of the nearby piano. Home-baked cookies are available for snacking, along with a variety of beverages. Guests may select a title from the bookshelves for reading fireside.

BED & BREAKFAST INNS OF BRITISH COLUMBIA

Morning arrives with a tray of coffee or tea, delivered to each room. Wander into the dining room for breakfast, to be enjoyed along with views of Duffin Passage and Clayoquot Sound. Wendy and Ralph visit with guests in the morning, while serving a top-notch meal. French bread pudding with strawberry sauce is one of Wendy's favorite dishes. European guests, not used to cornmeal, are wowed by cornbread, sauced with blueberries and served with Canadian back bacon. Wendy is sensitive to guests' allergies and dietary needs and can plan menus with these in mind, given advance notice. The challenge of gluten-free diets resulted in a savory quiche with a hash brown crust. Green chile omelets are another popular egg selection. Fruit juice and baked goods make daily appearances on the table as well. Wendy takes particular pride in the presentation of her cooking, often accenting plates with herbs and edible flowers from her garden.

Well-stoked and well-advised by their hosts, guests venture outside to discover Mother Nature's handiwork. A visit toThe Pacific Rim National Park Reserve is an excellent place to begin. Just shy of 200 square miles, the park is home to sandy beaches, dense old-growth rainforest, rocky headlands, fresh-water lakes and a multitude of wildflowers. Kayaking, surfing, diving and hiking are but a few activities available in the neighborhood.

Tofino has something to offer visitors year-round. Storm-lovers should visit in January, at the peak of winter's squalls. Mid-March brings a month-long Whale Festival, welcoming an estimated 19,000 Pacific gray whales, who cruise northward along the west coast of Vancouver Island to summer feeding grounds in Alaska and Siberia. Arts enthusiasts will enjoy a music festival in July and a performing arts festival in August. Local growers fete the oyster in November at the Clayoquot Oyster Festival.

Mediterranean Quiche with Hash Brown Crust

Serves 8

The potato crust is a tasty alternative to quiche's usual pastry crust, ans is suitable for those requiring a gluten-free diet.

Crust	3	cups shredded raw potatoes
	1/2	cup butter, melted
Filling	5	eggs
	1/4	cup diced onion
	2	tsp. butter
	1/2	cup grated cheddar cheese, preferably aged
	1/4	cup grated Monterey jack cheese
	1/4	cup crumbled feta cheese
	5	sun-dried tomatoes (not oil-packed), reconstituted in boiling water and diced
	1	tsp. dried oregano
	1	Tbs. chopped fresh chives or green onion tops
	1/2	cup milk
		salt and pepper to taste

Crust: Preheat oven to 425° F. Spray a 9" pie plate with vegetable spray. Press the potatoes into the pan to an even depth on bottom and sides. Pour butter evenly over potatoes and lightly salt and pepper. Bake 30 minutes. If crust seems to have shrunk in pan, reform with spoon. Crust can be prepared and baked one day before using.

Filling: Preheat oven to 350° F. Melt 2 t. butter in medium skillet and add diced onions. Sauté until translucent, but not golden. Set aside.

In a large mixing bowl, whisk together eggs until well blended. Add remaining ingredients and stir to blend. Carefully pour egg mixture into potato crust. Bake for 40-45 minutes or until center is set and a knife inserted comes out clean.

Remove from oven and serve immediately, garnished with fresh oregano leaves. Wendy serves this dish with sliced tomatoes and sautéed red, yellow and green peppers.

Oregon Bed & Breakfast Inns

Campbell House
Chanticleer Inn
Floras Lake House
Home by the Sea
Lighthouse B & B
The Lion and the Rose
Mattey House
Mount Ashland Inn
Portland Guest House
Portland's White House
Romeo Inn
Rosebriar Hotel
Sea Quest
Springbrook Hazelnut Farm
Steamboat Inn
Steiger Haus
Touvelle House
Tyee Lodge

How do they taste?
They taste like more.

H. L. Mencken

The Campbell House

252 Pearl Street
Eugene, OR 97401
Phone (541) 343-1119
Toll Free (800) 264-2519
Fax (541) 343-2258
E-mail: campbellhouse@campbellhouse.com
Web site: http://www.campbellhouse.com

High Season Rates: $86 - 350 (weekend) U.S.
Low Season Rates: $79 - $250 U.S.

The Campbell House

The Campbell House is akin to a phoenix rising from the ashes. Empty for fifteen years, the aging and decrepit house was purchased by the determined Myra and Roger Plant in 1991. The Plants had tried to buy the house five years earlier but were thwarted by an heir averse to the sale of his ancestor's home. Frustrated by her lack of knowledge in the transaction, Myra spent the intervening years acquiring her real estate license and subsequently entering the real estate business so that she would be prepared when the house came up for sale again. When it finally did, the Plants were ready.

The vacant home required an enormous amount of work to restore. While the structure was sound, the interior was a mess. Wallpaper hung in shreds on the walls, huge holes gaped in the floor, plaster was cracked and crumbling, and the building had been without a roof for several years. A contractor was hired to oversee the project and each weekend family and friends descended on the house for what turned out to be a two-year long work party. When guests visit Campbell House now, the only visible remnants of its former state are the photographs depicting the renovation, carefully organized into scrapbook form.

The inn's accommodations are a result of considerable research. Myra traveled extensively in her previous career and deliberately chose to stay in bed and breakfasts so she could get a sense of what worked and what didn't. What she discovered was that most b&bs were designed for the holiday traveler, not the business traveler, and thus, the corresponding amenities were absent. As a result, she chose to include televisions and VCRs, telephones with data ports, a desk, honorbar refrigerators, and luxury touches like terry robes, hairdryers, even ironing boards and irons. Fax and photocopy services, plus fitness club passes are also available.

The inn's thirteen rooms vary in size from small and cozy to spacious and elegant, each thoughtfully decorated and tastefully appointed. A new building, just opened in June, features three luxury rooms and two plush suites, all with jacuzzis and fireplaces, and decorated with exquisite attention to detail. Guests in every room will enjoy morning coffee and tea service, presented by miniature carved butlers and maids stationed outside each door.

The Campbell House serves breakfast from seven to ten each morning, allowing guests to dine at their leisure. Regulars demand that scones be served and other favorites include granola and mini Belgian waffles, along with a variety of egg dishes. Honeymooners can request their breakfast be served in bed. Special occasions, such as Mother's Day and the Christmas holidays, bring guests to the inn to enjoy high tea. Tables are dressed in white linen and arranged throughout the dining room, parlor and library. The inimitable beverage is served in antique English china cups along with plates of crumpets, scones, savory sandwiches and sweets. Private bridal teas can be booked with prior notice. Groups up to 125 can reserve the inn for weddings and receptions, while smaller groups may opt for the library as a private meeting room.

Eugene is Oregon's second-largest city, and home to the University of Oregon, which brings plenty of interesting events to town. Eugene also has its own ballet, opera and theater companies, offering a wide array of cultural diversions. Several good bookstores offer plenty of browsing while shoppers will find temptations at both the 5th Street Market and the Saturday Market – an outdoor craft fair ideal for checking out Eugene's enduring counter-culture. A number of wineries dot the rural area surrounding Eugene and Corvallis, providing ample touring and sampling opportunities.

Outdoor enthusiasts will find a surprising number of activities considering Eugene's urban locale. Canoeists and rafters can paddle either of Eugene's two rivers, the Willamette and the McKenzie, which run through town. Runners can pound Pre's Trail, named for famed long-distance runner Steve Prefontaine, stretching along the banks of the Willamette for six-plus kilometers. Hikers might find Spencer's Butte appealing, with its breath-taking views of Eugene and the two rivers.

Autzen Stadium is within walking distance of Campbell House, making it a popular overnight choice for football fans. Book early as foes of the Oregon Ducks fill up the inn on home-game weekends.

> The only way to keep your health
> is to eat what you don't want,
> drink what you don't like,
> and do what you'd rather not.
>
> *Mark Twain*

The Campbell House Scones

Makes 16

- 3 cups all-purpose flour
- 1/3 cup sugar
- 2-1/2 tsp. baking powder
- 1/2 tsp. baking soda
- 3/4 tsp. salt
- 3/4 cup (1-1/2 sticks) firm butter, cut into small pieces
- 3/4 cup chopped dried fruit or nuts (dried cranberries and hazelnuts are a favorite)
- 1 tsp. grated orange peel (optional)
- 1 cup milk
- cinnamon sugar (optional)

Preheat oven to 400° F. Lightly grease two baking sheets.

In a large bowl, mix together flour, sugar, baking powder, soda and salt, until thoroughly blended.

Using pastry blender or two knives, cut butter into flour mixture until it resembles coarse cornmeal.

Stir in the fruit, nuts or combination of both and grated rind if desired. Make a well in the center of the butter/flour mixture; add the milk all at once. Stir the mixture with a fork until the dough pulls away from the sides of the bowl.

With your hands, gather the dough into a ball; turn out onto a lightly floured board. Divide the dough into four parts and lightly pat each part into a round. Cut each round into 4 wedges and place on baking sheets.

Sprinkle with cinnamon sugar if desired and bake for 12 minutes or until golden. Serve warm with butter and jam.

Hazelnut Chicken Tea Sandwiches

Makes about 21 Finger Sandwiches

This recipe was created for the special teas at Campbell House by proprietor Myra Plant's sister, Sonja Cruthers.

4	cups shredded chicken
1/3	cup mayonnaise
1/2	tsp. salt
1/2	tsp. Cajun seasoning
1/2	cup hazelnuts, finely chopped (optional)
1	loaf McKenzie Farms brand Oregon hazelnut bread (if hazelnut bread is not available, choose another firm sandwich-type bread)

In a large bowl, mix together chicken, mayonnaise, salt, seasoning and hazelnuts, if desired. Taste and add mayonnaise and seasonings as desired.

Spread chicken salad evenly on a slice of bread. Top with another slice, trim crusts and cut each sandwich into three fingers. Repeat until filling and bread are gone.

Can be made ahead and frozen, or refrigerated with a slightly damp towel placed on top of sandwiches to keep bread from drying out.

Only dull people are brilliant at breakfast.

Oscar Wilde

Chanticleer Inn

120 Gresham Street
Ashland, OR 97520
Phone (541) 482-1919
Toll Free (800) 898-1950
Fax (541) 488-4810
E-mail: innkeeper@ashlandbnb.com
Website: http://www.ashlandbnb.com

High Season Rates: $135 - 170 U.S.
Low Season Rates: $75 - 95 U.S.

Chanticleer Inn

The original Chanticleer was a clear-voiced rooster in Chaucer's Canterbury Tale of Reynard the Fox. Ultimately, Chanticleer came to mean rooster and, roosters being the harbinger of morning, it seems an appropriate moniker for a bed and breakfast inn. This Chanticleer lives in considerably more comfort than Chaucer's medieval era would have allowed, on a quiet side street in Ashland, Oregon, a city famous for another well-known English writer.

The Craftsman-style house looks deceptively small from the street, yet offers visitors a choice of six guests rooms. The grounds drop sharply from the front of the house, opening up the rear to stunning views of the Cascades, Bear Creek Valley and the well-manicured gardens surrounding the inn. Koi swim in the garden's pond and the sounds of a small waterfall provide a soothing backdrop to a stroll among the flower beds or a seat on one of several patios.

Inside the inn, the living room is furnished with cozy chairs for curling up by the river rock fireplace. Wine, sherry and lemonade sit nearby for guests to sip fireside along with homemade cookies for munching. Morning light fills the east-facing dining room where guests congregate to admire the Cascade Mountain view and dine on Chanticleer's hearty breakfasts. Intriguing fruit preparations include cranberry-apple strudel, mango mousse tart and baked Oregon pears with brandy custard sauce. Guests rave about the artichoke strata, Dutch babies and Chanticleer's scrambled eggs with smoked salmon and herbs, served in pretty pastry cups. Fresh herbs from the garden season many a dish and make for attractive plate garnishes as well.

Chanticleer's quiet location belies its proximity to downtown Ashland. Just four blocks away, guests will find the main street, full of shops and restaurants, and Lithia Park, home to the outdoor Elizabethan Theater and its attendant Shakespearean productions. Not all entertainment is of the cultural sort. Ashland is rich in sporting opportunities as well. Skiing, fishing, river rafting, hot air ballooning and hiking can be had in the surrounding mountains and valleys. Pebby Kuan, Chanticleer's innkeeper, is an outdoor enthusiast and can assist with making reservations and recommendations for activities outdoors and in.

Ashland is also home to several fine restaurants and guests find the level of dining equal to that of much larger cities. Aficionados of French cuisine will find two delightful options in Monet and Chateaulin while die-hard Italian fans can be fulfilled at Il Giardino. Those interested in cutting edge fare should check out Firefly. Wine is a natural accompaniment to food and Ashland has a pair of wineries to inspect – Weisinger's and Ashland Vineyards.

Comfort awaits in one of Chanticleer's guest rooms. Aerie and Fleur offer the best views, along with sitting areas. Early risers can steal into the garden at first light from Rosette, Petelote and Jardin, each with its own private garden entrance. The main floor Maitre's French windows open to a view of the Cascades and garden. All rooms have queen beds and private baths. Aerie, Fleur and Jardin offer twin beds in addition to the queen. Other amenities include fresh flowers, robes, telephones and scripts from current Shakespeare Festival productions.

Northwest Eggs Supreme

Serves 4

- 4 frozen puff pastry cups
- 8 eggs
- 1 green onion, chopped
- 1/2 tsp. lemon thyme
- 4 oz. smoked salmon (not lox style), warmed
- 1 Tbs. butter
- parsley sprigs

Bake puff pastry cups according to package directions. Scoop out soft insides and discard.

Whisk eggs together, adding green onion and lemon thyme.

Melt butter in skillet over medium heat and add egg mixture. Scramble eggs to desired consistency.

Divide scrambled eggs into pastry cups and top with warm smoked salmon. Garnish with parsley sprigs. Serve immediately

---

The egg is to cuisine what the article is to speech.

Anonymous

Floras Lake House

92870 Boice Cope Road
Langlois, OR 97450
Phone (541) 348-2573
Fax (541) 348-2573
e-mail: floraslk@harborside.com
Website: http://www.harborside.com/home/f/floraslk/lakebnb.htm

Rates: $95 - 125 U.S.

Floras Lake House

An avid windsurfer, Will Brady discovered Floras Lake while attending the University of Oregon. Steady northwest winds off the Pacific Ocean, which can be seen from the lake, have made this body of water a sailor's mecca. A native of Palos Verdes, Will headed back to California after college, married and began a family. But a hectic lifestyle in the sprawling Southland wasn't what Will and his wife Liz wanted for raising children.

A friend suggested merging the Brady's love of windsurfing with the operation of a bed and breakfast – wouldn't Floras Lake be the ideal location? So, in 1991, they built a spacious home, with an apartment downstairs for the family and four rooms upstairs for guests, christening their new endeavor Floras Lake House. The inn, amidst native trees and a rolling expanse of green lawn, faces west with commanding views of both fresh water Floras Lake and the ocean. While Liz handles a lot of the b & b details, Will teaches their guests and others at his Floras Lake Windsurfing.

Beginners might want to rise early and hit the lake in the morning, when soft winds are more forgiving. By mid-day, breezes ranging from 15-25 knots blow across the water, more suitable for intermediate to expert sailors. Students can bring their own equipment or rent from Will, who has top quality rigs, ready to sail. The sandy bottom, warm (68 degrees) water, and shallow depth make the lake an ideal spot for pupils of all levels. Anyone feeling chilled by the outdoor exposure can retreat to the view sauna at the lake's edge. Windblown and sun-kissed after a day on the water, guests return to the house, shower, and head out in search of sustenance.

The town of Langlois, located on highway 101 east of Floras Lake, is small enough to qualify for the "blink and you'll miss it" tagline. It doesn't offer much in the way of restaurants, although it does have a top-notch windsurf and surf shop. Drive 17 miles north to Bandon, where hungry visitors can choose between several restaurants dishing out tasty and imaginative fare.

Back at Floras Lake House, snooze comfortably in the huge guest rooms, all with the same wide-open view of the lake and ocean. Of the four rooms, three sport king beds, perfect for stretching out those tired muscles. The fourth room has two double beds, a good family option. The South Room, with its centerpiece four-poster and the white wicker-accented North Room both have fireplaces. All rooms share two features – private baths and private deck entrances. Decks at several levels connect across the water view side of the house.

After a good night's sleep, guests assemble in the commodious living/dining room for breakfast. Twenty-foot high ceilings and a wall of windows ensure plenty of morning light. Hearty, healthy foods are served buffet-style from the adjoining kitchen area. Enjoy crunchy homemade granola, vanilla yogurt and a bowl of fresh fruit or berries, along with freshly baked muffins, sticky buns or French toast, maybe bagels and cream cheese. Homemade berry jams say summer all year long. On sunny mornings, enjoy breakfast on the deck, getting a head start on that tan.

Properly fueled, guests can partake of more than windsurfing. Boice-Cope County Park, home to Floras Lake, has a great trail system, accessible to runners, walkers, mountain bikers and horseback riders. This whole area is a little off the beaten path, so enjoy the solitude and revel in the natural beauty. And yes, relaxing on the deck or at the beach is always an option, too.

Aunt Bobbie's Sticky Bun Cake

Serves 12

This easily assembled recipe is prepared the night before serving.

1	bag Rhodes (or other) frozen dinner rolls
1	pkg. Jell-o ® Cook n Serve Butterscotch pudding mix
1/4	cup butter, melted
1/2	cup packed brown sugar
1/2	cup sliced almonds, chopped walnut or chopped pecans
2	Tbs. cinnamon

Butter bottom and sides of 9" x 3 1/2" bundt pan. Sprinkle nuts on bottom of pan and top with half the package of rolls (about 12-14).

Sprinkle dry pudding mix evenly over rolls. Mix together melted butter and brown sugar and pour over rolls. Sprinkle with cinnamon.

Cover, and let rise overnight in a cold oven or on countertop.

When ready to bake, pre-heat oven to 350° F. Bake for 18-25 minutes until golden and bubbling. Remove from oven, let rest for 2-3 minutes, then invert onto serving plate. Serve warm.

My wife and I tried to breakfast together, but we had to stop
or our marriage would have been wrecked.

Winston Churchill

Cranberry Muffins

Makes about 16 Muffins

Cranberry farming is a major industry on this stretch of the Oregon Coast. Other fresh or dried fruits and berries can be substituted, depending on the season or taste.

- 4 cups flour
- 2 cups sugar
- 4 tsp. baking powder
- 1 tsp. salt
- 1 cup butter, melted and cooled
- 1 cup milk
- 2 eggs
- 2 tsp. vanilla
- 1 cup fresh whole cranberries

Preheat oven to 400° F. Grease or spray muffin tins.

Combine flour, sugar, baking powder and salt in a large bowl, stir with a fork to blend.

In another bowl, mix together melted butter, milk, eggs and vanilla.

Make a well in the center of the flour mixture and pour in liquid ingredients. Stir until just blended. (Don't over-mix, it will make for tough muffins!) Fold in cranberries.

Spoon batter into prepared muffin tins.

Bake for 18-22 minutes, until golden and a toothpick inserted comes out clean.

A simple enough pleasure, surely,
to have breakfast alone with one's husband,
but how seldom married people in the midst of life achieve it.

Anne Morrow Lindbergh

The most memorable thing about my mother
is that for thirty years she served nothing but leftovers.
The original meal has never been found.

Calvin Trillin

Home by the Sea

444 Jackson Street
Port Orford, OR 97465
Phone (541) 332-2855
Email: Alan@homebythesea.com
Website: http://www.homebythesea.com

Rates: $85 - 95 U.S.

Home by the Sea

The tiny town of Port Orford, Oregon (pop. 1000) holds many surprises. Located 70 miles from the California border, Port Orford is tucked into a cove on this southern stretch of Oregon's coast surrounded by a bevy of natural wonders. The quiet streets belie the diverse amount of recreational activities, geographical superlatives and natural wonders that abound in the area.

How to find out what's here? Ask Alan Mitchell, proprietor of Home by the Sea. Alan not only knows the history of Port Orford (inadvertently named for explorer George Vancouver's friend, the Earl of Orford), but also the geography, the economics, the landmarks, the artists and recreational pastimes.

Residents of the area for many years, Alan and his wife Brenda designed and built Home by the Sea themselves. Sited on a bluff jutting into the cove, the house looks southward along the coast, offering guests an unusual vantage point from which to enjoy both sunrise and sunset. Looming below the house is Battle Rock, site of an historic clash between white settlers and Rogue Indians.

Guests can take advantage of the locale for beach-combing, fishing, windsurfing, bird- and whale-watching, and even pan for gold at the mouths of the Elks and Sixes rivers. Need some additional ideas? Alan can toss out travel ideas as quickly as flipping the morning's pancakes. His knowledge of the area extends far beyond the borders of Curry County. Visit "Oregon Coast Travel Tips Guidebook" available on the b & b's extensive website, www.homebythe sea.com. Alan offers travel tips by the milepost and has links to other sites of interest, plus loads of helpful hints for travelers.

Visitors will enjoy the homey dining room, papered with maps from the world over and decorated with works from local artisans. A trio of birds, including a striking peach-faced lovebird, serenades guests as they dine on honey-whole wheat waffles, French toast and organically grown strawberries along with locally produced syrups and jams.

Looking out the window, Battle Rock fills the foreground. Beyond is Humbug Mountain, the highest point on the Oregon coast. From the east, mature forest spills down the hillsides to the beach where sea stacks float along the coastline. Perhaps a pod of whales will swim by on their seasonal migratory tour. The phenomenal beauty of this area owes its pristine existence to geographic isolation. Developers have overlooked this serene seaside village, opting for more accessible sites north and south, resulting in a destination of great natural beauty and solitude.

Lost Bread

French toast is so good you forget how economical it is.
The French don't call this French toast. They call it *pain perdu*
or "lost bread" because it is a way to use up leftover bread
you would otherwise lose – the only bread you've got on
the baker's day off. French toast is actually better
if the bread is a little old or sliced and dried out overnight.

Marion Cunningham
The Breakfast Book

Home by the Sea Almond Eggnog French Toast

Serves 4

- 6 eggs
- 1 cup half and half
- 1/2 tsp. nutmeg
- 1 tsp. vanilla
- pinch salt
- 2 Tbs. brandy
- 1/2 cup slivered almonds
- 8 slices sesame seed French bread
- butter, for frying
- powdered sugar, for garnish

Whisk together eggs. Add half and half, nutmeg, vanilla, salt and brandy. Whisk well.

Pour into shallow baking dish and lightly dip each side of bread in egg mixture. Set aside.

Melt butter in a frying pan over medium-low heat until melted.

Add slices to fit without crowding. Cook first side, covered for 3 1/2 minutes, flip, sprinkle with slivered almonds and cook for another 3 minutes.

Lightly dust with powdered sugar and serve.

Lighthouse Bed & Breakfast

650 Jetty Road Southwest
P.O. Box 224
Bandon, OR 97411
Phone (541) 347-9316

Rates: $90 - 145 U.S.

Lighthouse Bed & Breakfast

There are five lighthouses dotted along the Oregon coast, casting their beams far out to sea to warn wary sailors. In Bandon-by-the-Sea, the Coquille River Lighthouse, built in 1896, occupies a unique location sitting on a finger of land overlooking the intersection of the river and the Pacific Ocean. Just across the river, on the inland side, sits Lighthouse Bed and Breakfast. One can imagine a string stretched across the river, connecting two tin cans placed against eager ears awaiting whispered code. Didn't Nancy Drew solve a mystery in a lighthouse?

The roomy contemporary home, with its weathered cedar face, fits perfectly into the beachy scene. A pile of fossilized rocks, collected on the beach a stone's throw away, greets guests as they climb up the stairs to the inn's entrance. A few of the rocks, their cracks visible, await the sharp impact that will split them open revealing their ancient secrets. Bandon is loved by rock hounds and beachcombers alike for the fossils, agates and jasper scattered across its beaches.

Shirley Chalupa, the owner and innkeeper, loves Bandon and her home by the sea. A holiday visit spawned the idea of "retiring" to this charming village. Thirty years in the hospitality industry made for a natural transition to the bed and breakfast biz.

Shirley is a gregarious hostess and packs a wallop in the kitchen. Her family-style breakfasts, served in the Great Room with a view of the inn's namesake, satisfy the heartiest of appetites. Fresh crab soufflé and shrimp quiche capitalize on the plentiful shellfish available along the coast, while cheeses from the local factory star in a variety of egg dishes. Add yogurt, home-fried potatoes and freshly baked muffins, and the makings of a feast are at hand.

After breakfast, a brisk walk into town is an ideal antidote to a full stomach. Bandon is an artists's colony of some repute. A leisurely stroll through Old Town should unearth the appropriate souvenir in one of the many galleries or shops. Stop in the Bandon Cheese Factory, not for cheese, but for ice cream. One scoop in the enormous waffle cone could put even the biggest fan of this frozen treat out of commission. Okay, buy some cheese. The extra aged white cheddar is delicious and packages of fresh curd are for sale too.

Laden with myrtlewood, blown glass and an antique trinket or two, return to the inn for a nap. Fortunate residents of the rooftop Gray Whale Suite can relax in the whirlpool, with views of river and beach from the large windows surrounding the tub. Don't worry about spectators – the lots on either side of the house are vacant. The California king bed invites sprawling and a wood stove heats things up. Downstairs are four more spacious rooms, each with a different view, queen bed and private bath. The Greenhouse Suite has a whirlpool for two, and though this one's lacking a view, there is a fireplace. Rested and refreshed, step out onto the beach to track down a fossil, peer across the horizon and watch for a whale or snap a photo of the sea stacks looming off shore. Breezes from the ocean will lift a kite and blow away any cobwebs remaining from that nap.

Shirley's Cheesecake

Serves 12

Innkeeper Shirley Chalupa believes everyone should have a good cheesecake recipe. This is her favorite.

Crust

- 2 cups graham cracker crumbs
- 6 Tbs. butter, melted
- 2 Tbs. sugar

Preheat oven to 350° F.

Combine crackers crumbs, melted butter and sugar thoroughly. Press crust evenly onto the bottom and sides of a 9" springform pan.

Bake for 5 minutes, remove from oven and make filling.

Cheesecake Filling

- 3 8-ounce packages cream cheese
- 1 cup sugar
- 4 eggs
- 2 Tbs. lemon juice
- 2 tsp. grated lemon rind
- 2 tsp. vanilla

In a large bowl, beat cream cheese until soft. Add sugar, blending thoroughly. Add eggs, one at a time, beating well after each addition. Mix in lemon juice, rind and vanilla.

Pour filling into prepared crust and bake for 35 minutes.

While cheesecake is baking, make topping:

- 2 cups sour cream
- 3 Tbs. sugar
- 1 tsp. vanilla

Blend together sour cream, sugar and vanilla.

Remove cake from oven and gently spread sour cream mixture over top. Return to oven and bake for an additional 12 minutes.

Remove from oven and let cool.

When thoroughly cool, fruit and glaze can be added. Lightly sugared strawberries or sliced peaches are excellent. Brush on bottled glaze (look for "Marie" brand) and let cake rest for at least another hour in the refrigerator before serving.

Blueberry Brunch Casserole

Serves 8

Enjoy this recipe at the peak of blueberry season or savor summertime in winter using frozen berries. The casserole is made the night before serving.

- 10 slices French-type white bread, crusts trimmed and bread cut into 1-inch cubes
- 8 oz. cream cheese (one package), cut into 1-inch cubes
- 1/2 cup blueberries (fresh or frozen), rinsed and drained
- 8 eggs
- 1/4 cup maple syrup
- 1-1/4 cup milk

Butter a 13" x 9" baking dish. Arrange half the bread cubes on the bottom of the dish. Scatter with cream cheese cubes and blueberries. Top with remaining bread cubes.

Continued on next page

Whisk together eggs, maple syrup and milk. Pour over bread. Cover pan with aluminum foil and chill overnight.

Remove foil and bake casserole at 350° F. for 30 minutes until puffed and browned. Cut into squares and spoon over the top:

Blueberry Sauce

- 1/2 cup sugar
- 1 Tbs. cornstarch
- 1/2 cup water
- 1/2 cup blueberries, fresh or frozen, rinsed and drained
- 1 Tbs. butter

In a small saucepan, stir together sugar, cornstarch and water over medium heat, stirring for 5 minutes or until thickened. Stir in blueberries, reduce heat, and simmer for 10 minutes.

Whisk in butter and stir until melted.

Serve over blueberry brunch casserole, French toast and pancakes at breakfast or over pound cake, shortcake or cheesecake for dessert.

If this is coffee, please bring me some tea.
If this is tea, please bring me some coffee.

Abraham Lincoln

The Lion & the Rose

1810 NE 15th Avenue
Portland, OR 97212
Phone: (503) 287-9245
Toll Free: (800) 955-1647
Fax: (503) 287-9247

Rates: $115 - 120 U.S.

The Lion & the Rose

Three friends, now business partners, restored this Queen Anne Victorian to its original magnificence through imagination, determination, eyes for detail and 15 layers of wallpaper. It took months, wading through the city bureaucracy for permits, applying for National Register of Historic Places status, replacing plumbing and electrical systems, adding air-conditioning, repainting, re-wallpapering, remodeling the kitchen. This labor of love and sweat equity belongs to Kevin Spanier, Sharon Weil and Kay Peffer, the proud owners and innkeepers of this elegant establishment known as The Lion and the Rose.

Kevin Spanier

Originally built in 1906 for brewery magnate Gustav Freiwald, the house and its outbuildings occupied three quarters of a city block. This provided stables, a playground for the Freiwald children and shelter for Mr. Freiwalds "horseless carriages," including a white Pierce-Arrow which was a regular on the Rose Festival parade route. The 18th amendment put an end to the brewery business and Mr. Freiwald's fortunes. Over time, the neighborhood changed. Apartment buildings now stand on some of the old Freiwald estate grounds. But the house still stands, 10,000 square feet of creature comforts and luxury.

The palette of the inn was determined by the National Register of Historic Places. It requires that buildings so designated use only colors in fashion at the time of the original construction. Thus, burgundies, deep teals and golds adorn the interior and meticulous care has been taken to recreate turn-of-the-century opulence. Plump sofas beckon guests, ornate plaster moldings adorn the ceiling, velvet draperies bedeck windows, bibelots and photographs sit cheek by jowl on tabletops. Surprisingly, amidst this riot of color, texture and pattern, an air of grace and elegance is maintained.

The grand table in the teal dining room is laid twice daily. In the morning, guests enjoy pastries and hot dishes along with fruit and fruit juices. Ginger-pear pancakes and baked strawberry or sour cream banana French toast are favorites. Savory dishes might include three-cheese quiche or a Spanish scramble accompanied by grilled bacon or sausage. In the afternoon, tea is served along with a selection of cakes, cookies and candy.

When guests retire to their rooms, they will again enjoy the attention to detail lavished on the main floor. Six rooms, each with a unique color scheme and antique furnishings, welcome weary visitors. The most popular room features a charming round cupola sitting area, which is the focal point of the inn from the exterior.

The three great friends (operating as TGF), work together to keep the inn operating smoothly. Kevin, an accountant by training and cook by design, spends most of his time in the kitchen. Kay, decorator extraordinaire, is the on-premise innkeeper. Sharon, a "people person" handles the sales and marketing side of things. This lively and irreverent trio has created a picture-perfect Victorian fantasy worthy of a visit.

The Lion & The Rose
Banana Sour Cream French Toast

Serves 8

The batter for this French toast can be made ahead and refrigerated until ready to use.

4	eggs
3/4	cup half and half
3/4	cup sour cream
1	banana
1/2	tsp. allspice
1	tsp. vanilla
16	slices extra-thick French bread

Place first six ingredients in blender. Blend until smooth and pour into large mixing bowl.

Dip each slice of bread into egg mixture and place on cookie sheet for 20 minutes.

Fry each slice in a non-stick pan until golden brown, flip and repeat. Serve hot with fresh sliced bananas for garnish.

I was so darned sorry for poor old Corky,
that I hadn't the heart to touch my breakfast.
I told Jeeves to drink it himself.

P. G. Woodhouse

Mattey House

10221 NE Mattey Lane
McMinnville, OR 97128
Phone (503) 434-5058
Fax (503) 434-6667

Rates: $90 - $110 U.S.

Mattey House

Inveterate globe hoppers, Jack and Denise Seed traded in their passports for plantings of pinot noir and placed themselves in Oregon's wine country, as the innkeepers of Mattey House. Now world travelers come to them, to enjoy the quiet countryside and easy access to the area's many wineries and restaurants.

The gravel drive leading to Mattey House borders four acres of vineyard planted to Muller-Thurgau grapes. The regimentally spaced rows of vines, marching from the drive to the house, create a dramatic foreground to the charming Queen Anne Victorian farmhouse. The gingerbread features so admired in this style of architecture are complemented by a simple color scheme of gray, blue and white. Small spots of color are provided by jewel-colored stained glass squares bordering windows.

Built in 1892, the house originally was home to an English cattle farmer. Already remodeled to accommodate bed and breakfast life when the Seeds bought Mattey House in 1992, the inn was closed during a transition period and re-opened to guests in 1993. Over time, Denise has made some changes to the house. The previous decor leaned towards dark colors and ornate, formal Victorian touches. Considering the simplicity of the house and its location, Denise chose to lighten the colors and give it more of a country feel.

The result: guest rooms in soft pastel hues, lace curtains at the windows and a light, airy feeling throughout the second floor where the rooms are located. Each of the four rooms is identified by a type of vinifera grape, with decor suited to the respective grape. The Riesling Room is the only one with a private bath. However, both the private and shared baths (there are two) sport old-fashioned claw-footed tubs and showers. On the main floor, the high-ceilinged parlor has comfortable seating scattered about the room. A cozy fireplace adds warmth in winter months. Stacks of books and board games lay about, awaiting the attention of guests. Emma, the resident English sheepdog, is a friendly companion to those missing pets at home.

In the morning, that eye-opening first cup of coffee can be enjoyed in the parlor, or sipped while perched on the front porch swing. In the afternoon, refreshments are offered, perhaps a glass of local wine along with tempting cheeses or silky pâté.

Family-style dining creates conviviality amongst guests at the breakfast table. Chilled baked peaches, bathed in cream and raspberry sauce could be a luscious beginning to the meal. Winter appetites are teased by fragrant baked pears, followed by a savory frittata or individual Dutch apple pancakes. Denise also enjoys baking scones, buttermilk raisin being her favorite.

Visitors interested in wine will appreciate Mattey House's location. There are a host of wineries nearby, providing several days worth of touring and tasting. At the end of the day, a visit to one of McMinnville's well-known eateries continues the theme since several have wine lists featuring local treasures not available in winery tasting rooms.

Pinot Noir is one of the premier grapes of this wine region. Every summer, Linfield College plays host to hundreds of burgundy lovers from around the world at the International Pinot Noir Conference (IPNC to those in the know). The conference fêtes the glorious grape with seminars, comparative tastings and winemaker dinners. Sold-out every year, conference attendees gain admission through a lottery (and a hefty ticket price). Planning to attend? Make lodging arrangements well in advance – rooms are as rare as spare tickets that week.

Chicken Liver Pâté

Makes approximately one cup

This quick and delicious hors d'oeuvre is served for afternoon refreshments at Mattey House, along with local wines.

- 8 oz. chicken livers
- pinch cayenne pepper
- 4 oz. butter or margarine, at room temperature
- 1/4 tsp. nutmeg
- 1 tsp. salt
- 1 tsp. dry mustard
- 1 clove garlic, finely minced
- 1/8 tsp. ground cloves
- 2 Tbs. onion, finely chopped
- 1 Tbs. brandy

In a medium saucepan, bring to a boil one quart water. Reduce heat, add chicken livers and simmer for 15-20 minutes. Drain and cool.

Chop chicken livers and place in blender. Add remaining ingredients. Blend until smooth.

Pack pate in a generous one cup mold or crock and chill overnight.

To serve, run a hot knife around pate and unmold onto serving plate or leave in crock for spreading. Garnish with herbs, and serve with sliced baguette, melba toasts or crackers.

To offer wine is the most charming gesture of hospitality,
and a host brings out for his guests the finest he has.
Whether there are four wines or one, the gesture is the same.

Alexis Lichine

Mt. Ashland Inn

550 Mt. Ashland Ski Road
Ashland, OR 97520
Phone (541) 482-8707
Toll Free (800) 830-8707
Fax (541) 482-8707
Email: Info@mtashlandinn.com
Website: http://www.mtashlandinn.com

Rates: $99 - 190 U.S.

Mount Ashland Inn

One of the best ways to experience southern Oregon's unique beauty is with a visit to the Mt. Ashland Inn. The inn is located eight miles south of Ashland and six winding miles up the mountainside. This sensational cedar lodge, hand-built from 275 trees on the surrounding property, sits amid evergreen forest, with expansive views of the Rogue Valley and the surrounding mountains, including Mts. McLoughlin and Shasta.

The four-story inn is reminiscent of a ski chalet, down to the peeled log beams and massive stone fireplace. Yellow cedar walls and Tiffany-style lamps cast a golden glow over the substantial plaid sofa and generous armchairs. Family mementos and heirlooms decorate the walls and mantel, creating a warm, friendly ambiance. Innkeepers Chuck and Laurel Biegert offer guests an enthusiastic greeting, echoed in the wagging tails of canine hosts, golden retrievers Aspen and Whistler.

The Biegerts purchased the inn in 1996. "It was love at first sight," says Laurel of their initial visit. Laurel grew up in Alaska, Chuck in Washington, and both are avid outdoor enthusiasts who especially enjoy the mountains, so the inn's location had distinct appeal. The Biegerts had been searching for an inn to buy, and discovered Mt. Ashland upon meeting the original owners at an innkeepers' conference.

Since their arrival, Chuck and Laurel have added amenities to the inn, increasing the casual luxury already present. A new, Finnish-style sauna cabin sits below the inn, partnered with an outdoor spa. Sitting in the spa at sunset, watching Mt. McLoughlin fade in the distance while clouds roll up the mountainside, is a delight not to be missed. Nearby is an observation deck, with rock fireplace and BBQ for picnickers. The Biegerts hope to add several freestanding cabins along an interpretive nature trail over the next couple of years.

The deluxe Sky Lakes Suite is another addition. The inn's top floor is devoted to this spacious retreat. Step through the log archway to bathing paradise for two in the spa tub, filled with water tumbling down the rock waterfall. Heavenly views, a dramatic river rock fireplace and king-size bed, along with the convenience of a mini-kitchen make for the plushest of accommodations.

Another suite, the Mt. McLoughlin, has its own sitting area, a king-size bed and marble-faced gas fireplace along with views of both it's namesake and Mt. Shasta. The Mt. Shasta Room has a spectacular view of it's namesake too, plus a queen bed and adjoining sitting area with daybed. The queen-bed-furnished Mt. Ashland and Cottonwood Rooms enjoy forest views. Each bed is topped with a handmade quilt, and all rooms are furnished with candles, a romantic and practical addition as the inn does experience power outages on occasion due to it's mountain-top location.

Power outages are a minor inconvenience considering the many attributes of the inn's location. Spring and summer guests can hike (or bike with inn-supplied mountain bikes) a portion of the Pacific Crest Trail which passes just above the inn. Aspen and Whistler are eager companions and trail guides. Birdwatchers will enjoy close-ups of hummingbirds, finches and jays as they visit the feeders Laurel has hung outside. Guests wishing to adventure beyond the mountain also will find plenty to do. Thrill seekers can ride the Rogue River aboard a jet boat, while the truly bold can elect whitewater rafting. Those less intrepid can enjoy a swim in the Rogue or Applegate Rivers. Golfers have twelve courses from which to choose in the Ashland/Medford area.

Winter might be the best time to experience the inn, when snow piles up and guests have the option of staying in, snug by the fire, or, venturing outdoors strapped to snowshoes and cross-country skis. Re-live childhood memories by flying across the snow on sleds and toboggans, or hit the slopes at nearby Mt. Ashland ski area, where downhillers have a choice of 22 runs, day and night, Thanksgiving through April. The road to the mountain is cleared on a regular basis, making both the inn and ski area very accessible during snow season

A hearty breakfast provides plenty of fuel for the day's pursuits. Chuck and Laurel serve two to three courses in the Mt. Shasta-view dining room. Guests settle into handmade Windsor chairs and tuck into dishes such as lemon zest French toast, served with homemade turkey sausage, or portabello mushroom frittata and smoked salmon focaccia. Creative fruit preparations often begin the meal; sparkling fresh peach soup with kiwi, warm spiced grapefruit topped with aromatic cinnamon or local pear cobbler with the surprise addition of crunchy granola. Anyone feeling a bit peckish between meals can plunder the stash of soup, popcorn, snacks and beverages, available to guests in the dining room.

Turkey Sausage

Makes about 25 Patties

3	lbs. ground turkey
3	Tbs. Dijon mustard
3	Tbs. Italian seasoning mix
1/3	cup soy sauce
1-1/2	tsp. garlic salt
1/2	tsp. freshly ground pepper
1/2	cup olive oil

Mix together all seasonings well and then add ground turkey meat. Mix by hand until well-blended.

Form sausage into cylinders about 3 inches in diameter and wrap in wax paper. Refrigerate overnight.

When ready to serve, slice cylinders into patties and fry over medium-high heat until cooked through inside and golden outside.

Mountain Almond Roca

A Christmas tradition in Laurel's family, but enjoyed anytime!

- 1 lb. butter
- 2 cups sugar
- 1 cup almonds, slivered, unblanched and unsalted
- 1 lb. high-quality semi-sweet chocolate, melted in double boiler over low heat
- 1 cup pecans, chopped

Cream together butter and sugar. Add almonds, stirring to mix.

Transfer mixture to heavy-bottomed saucepan and cook over medium heat, stirring constantly, until mixture reaches 290° F. on a candy thermometer. Immediately pour onto an 11" x 17" cookie sheet, spreading evenly.

Blot any butter that rises to surface and then spread half the chocolate over the hardening candy. Keep remaining chocolate warm in double boiler. Quickly sprinkle half the chopped pecans over the chocolate while chocolate is still warm.

When candy has cooled, turn over into another cookie sheet of same size or onto wax paper. Spread remaining chocolate onto candy and then sprinkle on remaining pecans.

Let cool until chocolate is completely hardened before breaking into pieces. Store in an airtight container, away from heat.

God made chocolate in heaven
and the devil gave it calories when it landed.

Unknown

Fresh Pear Cobbler with Homemade Granola

Serves 4

- 2 ripe pears, peeled, cored and sliced
- 1 tsp. lemon juice
- 1/2 to 3/4 cup homemade granola or commercial low sugar granola
- 4 ready to bake crescent rolls, cut into 1/2 " wide strips
- honey
- cinnamon sugar

Preheat oven to 375° F. Lightly spray baking dish with non-stick spray.

Mix together pears, lemon juice and granola, adding honey to taste if pears need some ripening. Transfer to baking dish and weave strips of dough across top. Sprinkle with cinnamon sugar as desired.

Bake for about 15 minutes, until dough is golden and pears tender.

Hot Smoked Salmon Spread

Makes about 2 cups

- 8 oz. smoked salmon, flaked or chopped
- 8 oz. cream cheese, at room temperature
- 2 Tbs. chopped yellow onion
- 1 Tbs. milk
- 3/4 Tbs. horseradish
- 1/4 tsp. *each* salt and pepper
- 1/3 cup slivered almonds

Preheat oven to 375° F. Combine all ingredients except almonds in a medium bowl and mix well. Transfer to baking dish and top with almonds. Bake for 10 minutes, or until heated through.

Serve hot with crackers or sliced baguette.

Portland Guest House

1720 NE 15th Avenue
Portland, OR 97212
Phone (503) 282-1402
Email: pgh@teleport.com
Website: http://teleport.com/~pgh/

Rates: $55 - 85 U.S.

Portland Guest House

In the northeast area of Portland lies the historic area of Irvington, one of the city's finest older neighborhoods. Many of the homes were constructed at a time when building was a craft and the finest materials were used to create a variety of architectural styles. Turn-of-the-century Victorians, stately Colonials and craftsman bungalows stand side-by-side in this eclectic area, and thanks to a mild climate and continued care from residents, most homes have retained their original character and condition.

The Portland Guest House (PGH), built in 1890, is a perfect example of the type of home visitors find in this neighborhood. The four-story house sits up off the street with a pleasing array of plantings filling the front yard. Eighteen months of remodeling resulted in a home accommodating seven guest rooms, eight bathrooms and an updated kitchen, while maintaining its original charm. The interior of the house is bright and light. Innkeeper Susan Gisvold describes the house as "working-class Victorian" and has kept the decor and furnishings simple and attractive to reflect this origin.

A collection of crisp white vintage and antique linens dresses everything from beds to tabletops, a fresh contrast to the dark, carved surfaces of the antique bedsteads, armoires and dining tables. Additional touches of white lace and bright quilts add color along with an interesting array of original artwork.

A professional home economist and mother of six, Susan Gisvold has turned her home management and cooking skills to the running of the bed and breakfast. Guests enjoy breakfast seated at individual tables in the dining room, or amongst the roses at garden tables in warm weather.

Susan describes her cooking as "fresh, wholesome foods of the Pacific Northwest." Popular amongst guests are the baked goods – brown sugar coffee cake, sour cream muffins full of chocolate chips or traditional French bread. In season, strawberries and blueberries are gathered fresh from the garden, along with savory herbs for seasoning omelets and other dishes. Homegrown pumpkins are magically transformed into delicious waffles slathered with local hazelnut butter.

The garden offers not only tasty additions to the table, but also a pleasant place to savor a glass of local wine or cup of tea. Old lilac trees surround garden furniture and gravel paths lead to beds full of seasonal flowers, fruits and vegetables. Rusted obelisks add architectural interest to the beds in winter and support vines of fragrant sweet peas in summer. If Portland's well-known rain prevents guests from being outdoors, then plenty of options are available via PGH's "Things to do when (not if) it rains" list.

Raining or not, one favorite activity is strolling Irvington's hip southern border, Broadway. Just around the corner from PGH, this busy one-way street is crammed full of trendy eateries, clever shops, bookstores and that Northwest requisite, coffee shops. Portland's efficient transportation system can quickly take visitors to other parts of the city. As "travel counselor," Susan happily offers suggestions for adventures in the city or day trips farther afield.

Life, within doors, has few pleasanter prospects than
a neatly-arranged and well-provisioned breakfast table.

Nathanial Hawthorne

Portland Guest House Pumpkin Waffles with Oregon Hazelnut Butter

Serves 5

Innkeeper Susan Gisvold uses pumpkins from her garden to prepare these popular waffles although canned pumpkin works equally well. Oregon is the premier producer of hazelnuts in the U.S. Hazelnut butter can be found in specialty food shops or easily made at home.

- 2-1/4 cups all-purpose flour
- 4 tsp. baking powder
- 2 tsp. ground cinnamon
- 1 tsp. *each* allspice and ginger
- 1/2 tsp. salt
- 1/4 cup firmly packed brown sugar
- 1 cup cooked pureed pumpkin or canned pumpkin
- 4 eggs, separated
- 2 cups milk
- 1/4 cup butter, melted

Preheat waffle iron. Stir together flour, baking powder spices, salt and brown sugar. In a separate bowl, combine pumpkin, egg yolks and milk. Add dry ingredients and melted butter to wet ingredients and stir to blend.

In a separate bowl, beat egg whites until soft peaks form. Fold into batter. Cook waffles according to waffle iron directions.

Serve with warm maple syrup and hazelnut butter.

Hazelnut Butter

- 1/2 cup butter, softened
- 1/2 cup hazelnuts, chopped
- 1/2 tsp. orange peel, grated

Combine above ingredients. Serve with waffles, pancakes or toast. Keep refrigerated.

Portland's White House

1914 NE 22nd Avenue
Portland, OR 97212
Phone (503) 287-7131
Toll Free (800) 272-7131
Fax (503) 249-1641
E-mail: pdxwhi@aol.com
Website: www.portlandswhitehouse.com

Rates: $98 - 149 U.S.

Portland's White House

Built in 1911 for a lumber baron at the record-breaking cost of $46,000, Portland's White House was the most expensive residence constructed in Portland at the time. Now listed on the National Register of Historic Landmarks, this regal home in Portland's historic Irvington District has been restored to its original grandeur and welcomes visitors as guests in one of it's elegantly appointed rooms.

The Italianate-style residence has a commanding entrance formed of double Corinthian columns which frame the heavy mahogany doors. The doors open into a wide entry hall decorated with hand-painted murals. Polished oak floors lead to the formal yellow drawing room with a regal grand piano, antique porcelains, bibelots and tasteful furnishings. Next door is the celadon-colored game room, its chess set awaiting a pair of players. More porcelains line the glassed-in shelves here, displaying the extensive collection of the innkeepers, Lanning Blanks and Steve Holden.

At the other end of the hallway sits the burgundy and rose-colored dining room, dominated by the grand dining table and impressive sideboard laden with blue and white porcelain urns, jars and vases. The table is graced by a lace cloth and formally set with china from the inn's collection of patterns. Each place setting is adorned with a crisp linen napkin, a product of the vintage mangle used on all the inn's table linens.

From the hallway, a massive staircase leads to the second floor guest rooms, softly lit by four opalescent Tiffany stained-glass windows. The upper floor is home to six guest rooms, all with private baths. The Canopy, Rose and Baron's rooms all have four-poster beds. The Balcony Room has access to the White House's decorative balcony while guests of the Garden Room enjoy a private veranda. The cozy Hawley Room has a queen-size bed and handsome armoire. Three additional rooms are housed in the newly remodeled carriage house, located just across the brick courtyard from the main house. Guests can choose from the Chauffer's Quarters with a striking king-size four poster bed and private Jacuzzi bath, the Carolina Room decorated with southern charm and a queen-size bed with goose-down comforter or the Blarney Room, named in honor of the previous innkeepers.

Innkeepers Lanning Blanks and Steve Holden welcome their guests with an abundance of charm and hospitality. A native South Carolinian, Lanning's warmth is omnipresent and his years of experience as an hotelier are evident throughout the house and guest rooms with touches like local handmade soaps, bottled water, plenty of thick towels, private telephones and data ports in all guest rooms.

Lanning's southern heritage also influences the menu with offerings of grits or fried mush with maple syrup. Rich butter pecan bread takes a turn as French toast, served with a dollop of whipped cream, satisfying any sweet tooth. Those who prefer savory dishes will enjoy Lanning's frittata, filled with caramelized onions and portobello mushrooms partnered with thick-sliced pepper bacon. Freshly squeezed tangerine or orange juices, fresh fruit and warm muffins, coffee cake or pastry complement the meal.

With advance booking, private dinners can be arranged at Portland's White House. Larger groups are welcome to rent the entire house including the black and white-floored ballroom on the lower level for wedding receptions and other affairs.

When one has tasted watermelons, one knows what angels eat.
It was not a Southern watermelon that Eve took;
we know it because she repented.

Mark Twain

Butter Pecan French Toast

Serves 8

Make the butter pecan bread the day before you plan to serve the French toast. The bread can also be enjoyed on its own as a tea bread.

- 2-1/4 cups all purpose flour
- 2 tsp. baking powder
- 1/2 tsp. baking soda
- 1/2 tsp. salt
- 1/2 tsp. cinnamon
- 1/2 tsp. nutmeg
- 1-1/3 cups firmly packed brown sugar
- 1 cup toasted pecans, coarsely chopped
- 1 egg, slightly beaten
- 1 cup buttermilk or heavy cream
- 2 Tbs. butter, melted

Preheat oven to 350° F. Grease a 9 x 5 x 3 loaf pan.

Sift together all dry ingredients except brown sugar. In a separate bowl, combine egg, buttermilk or cream, and melted butter, whisking to blend. Pour over dry ingredients, add brown sugar and chopped nuts. Stir just enough to moisten. Do not overmix.

Bake for 45-50 minutes. Let cool 10 minutes before removing from pan.

To make French toast, whisk together:

- 8 eggs
- 1/4 cup half & half

Melt 1 tablespoon butter over medium heat in a medium size skillet.

Slice butter pecan bread into 1" thick slices. Quickly dip each side into egg mixture (do not soak bread as it will fall apart) and place in skillet. Fry until golden, flip and repeat. Serve warm with maple syrup, whipped cream and toasted pecans

Caramelized Onion and Portobello Mushroom Frittata

Serves 8

1	medium red onion, thinly sliced
1	large ripe pear, peeled, cored and cut into 1/2" dice
1-1/2	cups portobello mushrooms, sliced 1/2" thick
1/4	cup fresh basil, coarsely chopped, plus additional sprigs for garnish
2	Tbs. balsamic vinegar
2	cups shredded parmesan cheese, divided
8	eggs
1/4	cup half and half
	salt and pepper to taste
2	Tbs. olive oil

Preheat oven to 350° F.

Heat olive oil in an 10"ovenproof skillet over medium heat. Add sliced onions and diced pear and saute until just soft, but not golden.

Meanwhile, whisk together eggs and half and half, seasoning to taste with salt and pepper.

Add mushrooms to skillet and continue cooking until any excess moisture has evaporated. Add chopped basil, stirring to mix. Pour over balsamic vinegar and cook until vegetables are lightly caramelized.

Turn the heat to low and sprinkle 1-1/2 cups grated parmesan over vegetables. Add the egg mixture, and top with remaining 1/2 cup grated parmesan. Remove skillet from stovetop and place in preheated oven. Bake for 20-25 minutes, until golden and center is just set.

Remove from oven, and let cool for 2-3 minutes. Loosen edges of frittata from pan with a spatula and place a cutting board large enough to cover over skillet. Invert to release frittata from skillet. Cut into wedges and serve immediately, garnished with fresh basil sprigs.

Alas! my child, where is the Pen
that can do justice to the Hen?
Like royalty, she goes her way,
Laying foundations every day,
Though not for public buildings, yet
For Custard, Cake and Omelette.
No wonder, child, we prize the Hen,
Whose egg is mightier than the Pen.

Oliver Herford

Romeo Inn

295 Idaho Street
Ashland, OR 97520
Phone (541) 488-0884
Toll Free (800) 915-8899
Fax (541) 488-0817
Website: http://www.opendoor.com/aaa-obbg/romeo.html

High Season Rates: $120 - 180 U.S.
Low Season Rates: $95 - $150 U.S.

The Romeo Inn

The Romeo Inn is aptly named considering its setting, just blocks away from the Oregon Shakespeare Festival's many theaters. Surprisingly, the inn was not christened in honor of the Bard's star-crossed lover, but for the original owners of the inn, Patty and Tony Romeo who transformed the private residence into a bed and breakfast in 1982.

The inn passed from the Romeos to another owner before Don and Deana Politis bought it in 1996. The Politis' had undertaken a two-year search through California, Arizona and New Mexico to unearth the perfect location for their new careers as innkeepers. Ultimately, they reached Ashland and Romeo Inn.

The Romeo Inn is a handsome Cape Cod style home with gracious rooms and a light, airy feel. Thick plum-colored carpet sets off pastel-colored furnishings. The inn is quiet and comfortable, with a distinct residential feel. A small library is tucked into one corner of the main floor, offering plush wing chairs for snuggling up with a book.

Lodgers at the Romeo Inn will find six spacious options from which to choose. Room names reflect Mr. Shakespeare's native England; Bristol, Coventry, Windsor and Canterbury, all with king beds and private baths (Bristol's is adjacent to the room), central air-conditioning and hand-stitched Amish quilts. The Canterbury and Windsor both have a day bed in addition to the king. Those wanting lots of elbow room might choose the blue and mauve Cambridge Suite featuring a dramatic vaulted ceiling and a pair of armchairs for lounging in front of the tiled fireplace, along with French doors leading to a private terrace. Separate from the main house is the Stratford Suite, decorated in shades of peach and teal. All the amenities needed for an idyllic holiday are here – views of the Cascades and Rogue Valley, whirlpool for two with a skylight view, a marble fireplace in the living room area and a full kitchen, ideal for self-catering romantics.

Each room has copies of scripts for current productions, handy primers for anyone brushing up on their Shakespeare. Notebooks entitled, "Essentials, Diversions and Enticements," are provided as well, offering suggestions for restaurants, activities and services in the area. Two diversions are located right in the inn's backyard; a swimming pool and spa, used year-round. Patio furnishings include two large umbrella tables and a hammock, swinging between two pine trees. The rear of the yard is highlighted by colorful perennial beds and Deana's cherished rose bushes.

Plentiful breakfasts will keep guests fueled through matinee performances. Deana gets raves for her scones, which she makes on a regular basis. Banana nut French toast is a favorite, too, along with spicy eggs Creole, served over polenta. Freshly squeezed orange juice and fresh fruit or melon keep the food pyramid from tipping over. The three-course meal is served in the sunny dining room, overlooking the pool and patio. Deana offers a light snack in the late afternoon to those returning from the theatre or other adventures. A refreshment area just off the patio is available for guests to help themselves to beverages and cookies throughout the day.

Ashland is theater-goers mecca. Deana tells of guests arriving on Friday afternoon, attending a play that evening, matinees Saturday and Sunday and a Saturday evening performance. The Oregon Shakespeare Festival performs plays mid-February through October. Nine other theater groups call Ashland home, offering comedy, musicals and experimental theater on a year-round basis.

Fans of the great outdoors will delight in Ashland's natural beauty. Mt. Ashland offers downhill and cross-country skiing. Golfers have a dozen courses to play in the area, while hikers and bikers will appreciate the miles of trails crisscrossing the acres of National Forest. Those with more leisurely pursuits in mind can stroll the streets of Ashland, perusing shops and galleries. The Festival of Light in December is a particularly beautiful time to visit Ashland when the city is lit by hundreds of thousands of tiny white lights and candlelit tours of selected homes are offered.

Cranberry Pecan Scones
Makes 16

4-1/2	cups all-purpose flour
1/2	cup sugar
2	Tbs. baking powder
1-1/2	tsp. salt
2-1/2	cups heavy cream
1	cup dried cranberries
1/2	cup pecans, chopped

Preheat oven to 425° F.

Combine dry ingredients in a large bowl and stir with a whisk to blend. Add dried cranberries and pecans, stirring to mix. Add the cream, mixing the dough by hand.

Divide the dough into two wax paper lined pie tins. Using the pan as a mold, press dough into shape and turn rounds out onto cutting board. Cut each round into 8 equal wedges and place on baking sheets.

Brush tops lightly with cream and bake for 15-20 minutes, until golden brown.

Remove from oven and cool on rack.

Rosebriar Hotel

636 Fourteenth Street
Astoria, OR 97103
Phone (503) 325-7427
Toll Free (800) 487-0224
Fax (503) 325-6937

Rates:
High Season: $70 - 135 U.S.
Low Season: $39 - 79 U.S.

Rosebriar Hotel

As the northernmost Oregon city on scenic US 101, Astoria is a common jumping-off spot for southbound tourists headed to the Oregon coast. It used to be that many folks were "just passing through," but the current vogue for Lewis and Clark, who camped at nearby Fort Clatsop in the winter of 1805-06, has put Astoria back on the map. Many a history buff comes to explore the town's rich history as the first permanent American settlement along the Pacific coast.

The Pacific Fur Company established a trading post here in 1811 called Fort Astoria after company founder John Jacob Astor, the Bill Gates of his day. Fur, an abundant supply of timber and fish, and proximity to the mighty Columbia River made Astoria a prosperous seaport, drawing adventurous settlers from the East coast and Europe to this little pocket of the Northwest Territories.

Prosperity continued into the 20th century through shipping, banking and other enterprises. Wealthy residents built grand homes overlooking the busy port and river. The most famous home in Astoria belonged to George Flavel, the town's first millionaire. Flavel House is now a museum, operated by the Clatsop County Historical Society, and is a fine example of the ornate and fanciful details so loved in Victorian architecture.

Several blocks from Flavel House stands another home of a prominent Astoria citizen. The three-story Georgian built by financier George Patton has passed through many incarnations since its birth in 1902. It remained a private home until 1950, when it was sold by Patton's descendants to the Catholic Church, which utilized the spacious residence as a convent. Thirty plus years later, it became Astoria's first bed and breakfast inn.

In 1992, the house came into the hands of the Tuckmans, local owners of a small lodging company. Realizing that the years had taken their toll, the Tuckmans closed what had been called Rosebriar Inn, and meticulously restored the home to its former beauty, reopening as the Rosebriar Hotel. The careful restoration received the prestigious Dr. Harvey Historic Preservation Award.

Called a small, classic hotel, the Rosebriar has ten comfortably furnished rooms in the main house and a carriage house adjacent. All rooms have a private bath and telephone as well as televisions tucked into armoires. Some rooms have views of the river and the spectacular Astoria-Megler Bridge, which stretches 4.1 miles across the Columbia from Oregon to Washington. The carriage house is a cozy spot for couples celebrating a special occasion. A gas fireplace, kitchenette and jetted tub provide all the amenities privacy-seeking sweethearts might need. For families or those less romantically inclined, the carriage house can sleep up to four.

A few remnants of the hotel's life as a convent are still visible. One of the guest rooms has a pretty plaster garland decorating the ceiling, the sole decoration allowed in the Mother Superior's quarters. The hotel's conference room was once the chapel. Subtly colored stained glass windows line the east wall and a dais at the south end of the room, backed by French doors leading to a private courtyard, functioned as the altar.

The wood-paneled dining room seats up to 32 guests at eight square tables. This is the domain of new chef, Anthony Tavoloni whose specialties include eggs Neptune – toasted english muffins layered with fresh shrimp and poached eggs, sinfully dressed in citrus hollandaise. Upside-down pancakes, with the heavenly fragrances of pear and vanilla tempt appetites many a morning. Crisp bacon, fresh from the local butcher and oven-baked, has been known to draw sleepy guests out of bed early. Baked goods are made fresh in-house and menus rotate on a seasonal basis. New menu items are expected as Chef Tavoloni settles in.

History awaits outside the front door. Don a coonskin cap and head up Coxscomb Hill to the Astoria Column. The 125-foot tower, decorated head-to-foot with a handsome sgraffito frieze, was built to commemorate westward migration and discovery. Portraits of Meriwether Lewis, fellow explorer William Clark and their sponsor, Thomas Jefferson are scratched into the clay surface. Climb up the 164 stairs inside the tower and be rewarded with a view up the Columbia to Washington State and southward along the Oregon coast, where on a clear day it's reported that the Cape Meares Lighthouse at Tillamook is visible.

Finnish Pancakes

Serves 6

There is a large Scandinavian population in Astoria, originally drawn here by plentiful fishing and logging. A local Finnish family has handed down this recipe for four generations.

8	eggs
1/4	cup honey
2-3/4	cups milk
3/4	cup flour
1/4	cup butter
	marionberry syrup
	crème fraiche
	fresh mint sprigs

Preheat oven to 450° F. Place a 12" ovenproof skillet in the oven to heat. Whisk together eggs, honey and milk. Add flour and whisk again to blend.

Remove skillet from oven and reduce heat to 400° F. Melt butter in hot skillet and pour egg mixture into skillet.

Bake for 10 minutes, then reduce heat to 350° F, flip pancake in skillet and bake for an additional 15 minutes until puffy and golden. Remove from oven, let rest 2-3 minutes and cut in wedges to serve. Top with marionberry syrup and crème fraiche, garnish with a mint leaf.

Sea Quest
Bed & Breakfast

95354 Highway 101
P.O. Box 448
Yachats, OR 97498
Phone (541) 547-3782
Toll Free (800) 341-4878
Fax (541) 547-3719
Email: seaquest@newportnet.com
Website: http://www.seaq.com

Rates: $135 and up U.S.

Sea Quest Bed & Breakfast

A quest is defined as the act or instance of seeking or pursuing something – a search. Beach lovers on a quest for the road less traveled should head to the southern half of Oregon's coast. The traffic and crowds so prevalent on the northern coast thin out and greater distances stretch between towns. The vista seems wilder, even desolate, particularly when seen through a mist of rain. This is where the mighty Pacific Ocean meets the emerald-green Siuslaw National Forest, a dramatic landscape where thundering waves crash at the feet of rocky, timber-capped slopes.

Cruising down 101, in pursuit of the spirit of that infamous road, a nostalgic panorama of old-fashioned motels and care-worn beach cottages flashes by. Their weathered, salt-sprayed countenances bring to mind a scrapbook filled with pictures of summers past - sand castles, sunburn, beach blankets and Kool-Aid. Charming as these mental snapshots may be, they also conjure memories of thin mattresses, threadbare sheets and pebbly upholstery on second-hand sofas, standard issue furnishings for many rustic beachside hostelries.

Travelers looking for lodgings with memorable charm, but more urban comforts would do well to seek Sea Quest Bed and Breakfast. Steer south to Yachats (Yah-hots) a quiet, arts-oriented hamlet folded around a curve of beach and backed by acres of evergreens marching heavenward. Sea Quest is few miles further south, on a shallow bluff overlooking Ten Mile Creek and many more miles of ocean.

From the terra-cotta tiled lobby, follow the signs upstairs where hosts George and Elaine Rozsa welcome guests amidst an *Alice in Wonderland* meets *Country Living* atmosphere. Elaine is a collector of "stuff" and displays an extraordinary talent creating vignettes with her collection that delight the eye and gladden the heart.

A crackling fire in the brick-faced hearth demands cozying up in one of the overstuffed chairs or sofas. There are books and magazines aplenty for the casual or serious reader. Have a cup of tea, and snack on poppyseed bundt cake or home-baked cookies, as you gaze at the view through windows trimmed with garlands twinkling with tiny white lights. While away the hours piecing together a jigsaw puzzle or commandeer fellow guests into some friendly competition at one of the game tables.

Head outdoors for a stroll across the lawn and a hop down to the beach, littered with driftwood and shells. Generous gusts off the ocean make for ideal kite-flying conditions or a wind-whipped horseback ride. In town, two good choices for gallery browsing, Earthworks and Backporch Gallery, offer quality works from local artists, including pottery, woodwork, glass and jewelry. Anglers will enjoy smelt fishing April through October, when the silvery fish come to shore to spawn. Yachats is one of the few spots on the globe where the sardine-like smelt congregate for this purpose.

Superlatives abound on this coastline, and one lies just south of Sea Quest on Highway 101. One of the highest points on the Oregon coast, Cape Perpetua, stands 800 feet above sea level. The promontory is a great place to drink in the kaleidoscopic Pacific and get a sense of the immense powers of Mother Nature. The Visitor's Center shows a film dramatizing the forces that created the Oregon coastline, along with housing various maps and displays familiarizing visitors with the ecological and anthropological history of the area.

THE GOURMET'S GUIDE TO NORTHWEST BED & BREAKFAST INNS

After a day buffeted by the forces of nature, a soak in the whirlpool tub might be just the ticket. Pad across the soft carpet to the snug bed with its nest of pillows, lean back and enjoy the continuous sound of the waves, background music around the clock. Each room enjoys a private entrance from the beach, with a small porch perfect for collecting seaside treasures. Elaine's imaginative sense of decor turns up again, be it bent willow furnishings, vintage crates holding soaps or colorful contrasting fabrics dressing beds, windows and furnishings.

More clever ideas pop up at breakfast. Served buffet style, from the tiled kitchen counter, guests get their first eye-opener when pouring their morning juice into glasses presented in an antique suitcase! Mugs for coffee and tea are stacked nearby. When breakfast is ready, warm plates are offered, and guests help themselves to an array of choices; seafood salad-stuffed croissants, homemade granola (presented with conch shell for scooping), warm pear pecan coffee cake, crêpe casserole, and fresh fruit. Bright salad greens partnered with vinaigrette or a lush platter of sliced tomatoes, cucumbers and avocado are a surprising and refreshing menu selection. Dine in candlelit comfort at one of the cheerfully outfitted game tables, enjoying the ever-changing view outside.

"A loaf of bread," the Walrus said, "Is chiefly what we need;
Pepper and vinegar besides are very good indeed.
Now if you're ready, Oysters dear, we can begin to feed."
But answer there came none –
And this was scarcely odd because they'd eaten every one.

Lewis Carroll
The Walrus and the Carpenter

Orange Poppyseed Bundt Cake

Serves 14

This delicious cake makes a great addition to the breakfast table or tea table.

1	cup butter
1-1/2	cups sugar
4	eggs
1	cup sour cream
1	T. grated orange peel
1/2	cup orange juice concentrate
1/3	cup poppy seeds
2-1/2	cups flour
1	tsp. baking powder
1/2	tsp. baking soda
1/2	tsp. salt

Preheat oven to 375° F. Spray a 9" x 3" bundt pan with cooking spray.

In a large bowl, cream together butter and sugar. Add eggs, sour cream, orange peel and concentrate, beating until smooth.

In a medium bowl, mix together dry ingredients. Stir dry ingredients into wet ingredients until just combined.

Spoon into prepared bundt pan and bake 55-60 minutes. Cool 5-10 minutes before unmolding.

When cake has cooled, drizzle over:

Orange Glaze

2	cups powdered sugar
1/4	cup orange juice concentrate
10	mandarin orange slices, chopped *or*
2	Tbs. marmalade
1/2	tsp. grated orange zest

In a medium bowl, whisk together ingredients until smooth, adding warm water if necessary, until desired consistency is reached.

Coffee should be black as hell,
strong as death,
and sweet as love.

Turkish Proverb

Springbrook Hazelnut Farm

30295 N. Hwy. 99 W
Newberg, OR 97132
Phone (503) 538-4606
Toll Free (800) 793-8528
Fax (503) 537-4004
Email: Ellen@nutfarm.com
Website: http://www.nutfarm.com

Rates: $90 - 150 U.S.

Springbrook Hazelnut Farm

An artists eye is evident at Springbrook Hazelnut Farm. Colors, vivid and bright, enliven each room. The same brilliant yellow used by Claude Monet in his house at Giverny is used in the 40-foot long center hall. The lemony hue glows in the living room as well, punctuated by persimmon-colored slipcovers on chairs and glossy white woodwork framing doorways. The artist is innkeeper Ellen McClure. Her works and that of other artists hang on the walls and decorate tabletops.

Ellen and her husband, Charles, were inspired to convert their home into a bed and breakfast after enjoying country inns in Ireland. The 1912 Craftsman-style home began life as Orvania Farm, so named by the Pennsylvania farmer who settled here in the early part of the century. The property now takes its name from the 60 acres of hazelnut orchards surrounding the estate.

At Springbrook Farm, the fertile soil of the Willamette Valley nourishes the hazelnuts and more. A perennial garden blooms around the back porch. Tomatoes, corn, peppers, herbs and carrots create a colorful and tasty palette in the vegetable garden. Old-fashioned irises and grasses surround the pond where a canoe awaits guests for a pleasant paddle across the smooth surface.

Breakfast is prepared in the retro green and ivory kitchen. Glossy marlite, a surfacing material from the 40s that imitates marble, covers the ceiling and walls. A vintage Spark gas stove and oven are used for cooking. In the center of the kitchen stands a chopping block, its well-worn surface testament to a former life in a meat-packing plant. One can see the artist here as well. An easel rests at the far end of the kitchen, displaying a work in progress

The morning meal is served in courses, either in the fruitwood paneled dining room or on the white wicker-filled sun porch with its green and white checkerboard floor. Menus vary, according to the season, and utilize products from the Farm or the local area. Hazelnuts make a showing in baked goods and granola. Zucchini and herbs from the garden enhance a frittata. Another favorite is crêpes, full of Black Forest ham and asparagus, drizzled with hollandaise. In summer months, fresh fruit from local farmers abounds with offerings of luscious berries, nectarines, peaches and plums.

The main house features four rooms and also on the grounds are a refurbished carriage house and charming cottage. All buildings on the estate are listed on the National Register of Historic Places. Each room is thoughtfully decorated, with a successful mix of the old and new. Both the carriage house and cottage have kitchens, and guests can select produce from the garden when preparing meals. The grounds also offer a swimming pool and tennis courts. A walk through the hazelnut orchard leads guests to the neighboring winery, one of many in the area.

Life is a great big canvas,
and you should throw all the paint on it you can.

Danny Kaye

Springbrook Hazelnut Farm Hazelnut Granola Parfaits

Serves 4

Hazelnuts and berries are two products for which Oregon is renowned. In this recipe the granola is layered with berries or other fresh fruit and yogurt for the first course of a full breakfast. The parfaits also would be perfect alone for a light breakfast.

Hazelnut Granola

Mix together in a large heatproof bowl the following:

- 6 cups oatmeal
- 1 cup chopped hazelnuts
- 1/2 cup chopped walnuts
- 1/2 cup sunflower seeds
- 1/2 cup slivered almonds
- 1/4 cup oat bran
- 1/4 cup wheat germ

Preheat oven to 325° F. In a medium-sized saucepan, mix together:

- 1/2 cup brown sugar
- 1/4 cup molasses
- 1/4 cup honey
- 1/4 cup apple juice
- 2 Tbs. hazelnut oil (or substitute any vegetable oil other than olive oil)

Combine above ingredients and bring to a boil over medium heat. Pour over granola and mix well. Spread granola on baking sheets and bake for 40 minutes until lightly browned, stirring often. Let cool and store in airtight container. Makes approximately 8 cups of granola.

To make parfaits:

- 2 cups fresh fruit (raspberries, blueberries, nectarines, etc.)
- 2 cups lemon yogurt (substitute with other flavors or plain)
- 2 cups hazelnut granola
- 4 8 oz. stemmed glasses

In each glass, layer 1/4 cup fruit, 1/4 cup yogurt and 1/4 cup granola. Repeat. Garnish with fresh mint leaves.

Steamboat Inn

42705 North Umpqua Highway
Steamboat, OR 97447-9703
Toll Free (800) 840-8825
Fax (541) 498-2411

Rates: $125 - 235 U.S. (March - November)

Steamboat Inn

Oregon's fast-moving North Umpqua River runs through miles of the Umpqua National Forest, home to ancient stands of western hemlock and Douglas fir. Anglers the world over come here for top-notch fly fishing. Standing streamside, with the icy waters of the river rushing by, fisherman can while away the hours casting for steelhead. When the light fades, fishermen reel in their lines and head for camp. Savvy fisher folk know the best place to "camp" is Steamboat Inn.

Steamboat is the unique creation of Jim and Sharon Van Loan, proprietors since 1973. An oasis of civility on the rustic riverbanks of the North Umpqua, this country inn began its life as a general store. The general store is now the lobby/dining room/fly shop, but a sense of rural commerce still pervades its warm wood walls. The Van Loans have expanded Steamboat considerably over the years to accommodate the increasing number of fly fisherman flocking to the river, all the while maintaining a high level of hospitality. Loyal guests return year after year to fish the river and enjoy the comforts of Steamboat.

Fishing isn't the only draw to Steamboat. The inn has established a reputation for fine cooking, and caters to guests, locals and travelers throughout the day in the café. Opening at eight in the morning, the café serves breakfast all day so diners can enjoy Steamboat's signature salmon hash on toast, sour cream roll ups filled with strawberry rhubarb jam or decadent praline French toast filled with ricotta, regardless of the hour. Eggs, granola and traditional breakfast sides are available for simpler appetites. Savory homemade soups and breads are offered at lunch along with a variety of salads and housemade desserts.

The café closes at six so veteran manager Pat Lee and her staff can shift their focus to Steamboat's famous family-style dinners, served on the massive sugar pine slab tables in the dining room. The dinner hour varies according to season, being served one half hour after last light so ardent fishermen can savor every last moment on the river. Those staying at the inn and folks with reservations gather in the library for an aperitif and hors d'oeuvres, then move to the dining room to feast on organic greens, local lamb, pork or game, a selection of side dishes and homemade breads all washed down with Oregon wines. The inn is noted for its extensive list, specializing in Northwest wines. An annual wine dinner series each spring showcases the talents of Northwest winemakers and guest chefs.

After dinner, guests slip away to riverside cabins, just below the inn, serenaded by the rushing river. The cabins feel properly rustic with pine paneling, comfortable furnishings and small decks overlooking the river. Cabins 7 & 8 sit above Maple Ridge Point, where western author Zane Grey once camped. Two suites enjoy river views plus gracious living rooms with wood-burning fireplaces and deep, Japanese-style soaking tubs. One half mile upstream, five cottages are tucked into the woods, each complete with kitchenette, deck, fireplace, soaking tub, king bed and sleeping loft, perfect for two couples or a family. Fully furnished accommodations are available at Camp Water Houses, a group of three-bedroom, one bath homes, replete with kitchens and washers and dryers – well-suited to longer stays.

First time fishermen, or those looking for expert tips, can retain the services of guides and drift boats through the inn. Steamboat is in the middle of thirty-one miles of "fly-fishing only" water and has all the supplies needed for fishing the North Umpqua in their fly shop. Sportsmen looking to outfit themselves in advance can contact the inn for suggested equipment.

Alternative activities include hiking the many trails in the Umpqua National Forest, swimming in the river, or a visit to Crater Lake National Park, southeast of Steamboat, home to the nation's deepest lake. A 33-mile drive around the perimeter of the lake offers fine views at several lookout points. Wine lovers will want to visit the eight wineries in the Roseburg area, which make up Oregon's Umpqua Valley appellation.

Salmon Hash

Serves 6

- 1 1/2 lbs. marinated salmon (marinade recipe follows), filleted and cut into 1oz. pieces
- 2 lbs. red potatoes, cut into 1/2" dice and parboiled
- 1 cup red onion, julienned
- 1/2 cup red bell pepper, julienned
- 1 cup asparagus, broccoli or green beans, cut into 1-2" pieces
- 2 Tbs. olive oil
- salt and pepper to taste
- 6 slices sourdough or rye bread, toasted
- lemon dill yogurt sauce (recipe follows)
- chives, for garnish

Prepare salmon marinade, add salmon and refrigerate overnight. Prepare lemon dill yogurt sauce and refrigerate.

Preheat oven to 400° F.

In a large saute pan, heat olive oil over medium high heat. Add onions and potatoes, and saute until potatoes are crisp, about 10 minutes. Stir in bell pepper and asparagus, cook for 1 minute. Remove pan from heat, cover and set aside.

Remove salmon from marinade and place on lightly oiled baking sheet. Place in oven and bake for 7-10 minutes, depending on how well done you prefer your salmon. While salmon is baking, toast bread.

Place one piece of toast on each plate. Stir the potato mixture, adding salt and pepper to taste. Spoon potato mixture equally over each piece of bread, creating a mound. Remove salmon from the oven and divide evenly on each potato pile. Drizzle with lemon dill yogurt sauce and garnish with fresh chives.

Salmon Marinade

(will marinate up to 2 pounds fish)

- 2 Tbs. vegetable oil
- 1 1/2 Tbs. soy sauce
- 1 Tbs. lemon juice
- 1 clove garlic, minced
- 1/4 tsp. dried thyme

Combine all ingredients in a small bowl and whisk until well combined. Pour over fish.

Lemon Dill Yogurt Sauce

> 1 cup plain yogurt
> 1/3 cup mayonnaise
> 2 Tbs. lemon juice
> 1 Tbs. horseradish
> 2 Tbs. fresh chopped dill
> salt and pepper to taste

Combine all ingredients in a small bowl and whisk for 1 minute. Serve immediately or refrigerate for later use.

Cinnamon Orange French Toast with Vanilla Ricotta Stuffing

Serves 4

> 8 thick slices good egg bread

Vanilla Ricotta Stuffing

> 1 cup ricotta
> 2 tsp. vanilla
> 1/3 cup powdered sugar
> 1 Tbs. water
> 2 Tbs. hazelnut praline*, finely processed

Cinnamon Orange Egg Wash

> 1 cup heavy cream
> 6 eggs
> 1/3 cup freshly squeezed orange juice
> (use one whole orange for juice and zest)
> 1 Tbs. grated orange zest
> 1-1/2 tsp. ground cinnamon
> 1/3 cup powdered sugar
> 2 Tbs. butter
> 2 Tbs. hazelnut praline*, finely processed
> 1 Tbs. grated orange zest
> 1/2 cup whipped cream

Continued on next page

Zest, then juice, orange, setting zest and juice aside.

Make the stuffing; Combine sugar, vanilla and water in a small bowl. Stir until smooth. Add the ricotta and stir to blend. Fold in the processed praline and set aside.

Make the egg wash: Whisk together cream, eggs, orange juice, zest, cinnamon and powdered sugar. Pour into an 8" x 8" square pan.

Generously spread ricotta stuffing evenly on two slices of bread and put together to make a sandwich. Repeat with remaining bread.

Heat a skillet large enough to hold all the French toast over medium high heat, add the butter to melt.

Whisk the egg mixture in the 8 x 8 pan (cinnamon and orange zest will fall to bottom of pan; whisk before dredging each sandwich)

Place French toast into egg mixture and let soak for a few seconds on each side, being careful not to let it get too soggy.

Place in skillet, reduce heat to medium and cook for about 3 minutes on each side, or until golden.

Remove from skillet and cut each sandwich in half. Arrange two halves on a plate, garnish with a dollop of whipped cream, a little orange zest and a generous sprinkle of the remaining praline.

* Make your own hazelnut praline or buy it already made. Peanut brittle or almond roca (without chocolate) works well too. Place praline in a food processor and pulse until broken up then process until finely chopped. A total of 4 oz. praline is needed for this recipe.

Steiger Haus

360 Wilson Street
McMinnville, OR 97128
Phone (503) 472-0821

Rates: $70 - 130 U.S.

Steiger Haus

Just a stone's throw from the pretty Linfield College campus and historic downtown McMinnville is Steiger Haus, perched on a steep slope overlooking Cozine Creek. From the street, the cedar-shingled house appears compact, even small. Walk into Steiger Haus, however, and discover three spacious stories stacked up against the hillside.

The distinctive look of this house is the result of its precipitous location. Carefully laid out by the previous owner, city planner Lyn Steiger, it is cleverly designed to take advantage of its unusual plat. Viewed from the terraced gardens below, the home appears in shape like an English Tudor, but with an effect more Swiss chalet.

Susan and Dale DuRette purchased Steiger Haus from the retiring owners in 1996. Committed to maintaining the quality established by the previous innkeepers, the DuRettes also have added of few of their own touches during their tenure. A nod to the area's (and guests') passion for wine is apparent in accents of burgundy and deep green, and grape cluster-bordered wallpaper. Handcrafted grapevine wreaths and swags decorate many rooms. The house has a pleasant, Northwest feel, with lots of wood accents and plenty of light from the many windows stretched across its southern face.

The main level is a common area, including a sitting room and the kitchen/dining area where Susan serves up what she describes as "Mom food" to her guests, utilizing indigenous products whenever possible. This translates to hazelnuts in pancakes, peaches or strawberries in crêpes, kiwis atop French toast and tangy Tillamook cheddar melting atop artichoke bacon frittatas with sweet peppers. The smoky bacon is sent over by the local packinghouse along with flavorful sausages. Those famous Oregon berries arrive hot and juicy under their blanket of batter in cobblers. Diners gather around a common table to enjoy home-style cooking and one another's company. Jays, housewrens and chickadees flit outside the window, picking up their breakfast from the several bird feeders hanging close by.

Star-struck guests might choose a room on the garden level – Zsa Zsa Gabor slept here. Two rooms and a suite comprise this level, with the suite offering a television and brick fireplace. The addition of a conference room makes this area handy for small groups to meet. Grape geeks, take note – Robert Parker, Jr. slept upstairs in the Treetop Suite. Maybe he gazed out the bay window to admire the tall stands of trees or pondered the next edition of his newsletter while relaxing in the soaking tub. Next door is the Rooftop Suite, with a pair of twin beds. Booked together, these two suites with their shared TV/sitting room, create a private area for families or a group of friends traveling together.

Step outdoors onto one of the many decks wrapping Steiger Haus. Breathe in the fresh air, scented by pine, cedar and fir. Sit quietly and perhaps a deer will stop near the creek to munch on tender leaves. The landscape is pure Northwest, filled with Oregon grape, salal and rhododendrons. Magnolias and dogwoods brighten the view in spring.

A pleasant five-block stroll away are tempting restaurants and shopping. Hop in the car, and cruise up and down 99W in search of that perfect wine. There are enough wineries and tasting rooms in the Yamhill County area to keep enophiles busy for a week. Roadside stands sell Oregon hazelnuts and walnuts, in the shell or incomparably tasty freshly-shelled meats. Fruits and berries, by the bushel and flat, create colorful displays in season. During the winter, pick up jams, syrups and other treats from local farms to take home for lucky friends and family.

Kiwi-Banana French Toast

Serves 8

Most folks think of kiwis as a tropical fruit. However, it grows best in temperate climates like Oregon, where the plant enjoys a dormant period and a long growing season. The micro-climate in the Dundee Hills has proven ideal for kiwi production. The fruits ripen in late fall.

6	kiwi fruit
3	bananas
1/3	cup kiwi syrup (see note)
7	eggs
1-1/2	cups milk
1	tsp. vanilla
1/4	tsp. nutmeg
16	thick slices (about 1") French bread

Preheat oven to 300° F.

Peel kiwis and bananas and slice into 3/8" thick rounds. Place in a bowl and pour kiwi syrup over the fruit. Set aside.

Whisk together eggs, milk, vanilla and nutmeg. Dip bread slices into egg mixture and let soak about 30 seconds per side.

Melt a small amount of butter or margarine on a griddle or in a skillet. Cook bread over medium heat, 2-3 minutes per side or until each side is golden brown. Add butter or margarine to the pan as needed to cook remaining slices.

Keep cooked slices of French toast warm in the oven until remaining slices are done.

To serve, place two slices of French toast on each serving plate, spoon kiwis and bananas over toast. Sprinkle with powdered sugar if desired.

Note: Kiwi syrup can be purchased or made as follows: mix together 1 cup water, 1/2 cup sugar and 4 kiwis, peeled and chopped. Cook in a non-reactive saucepan over medium heat until thick. Makes about 1 cup.

Touvelle House

455 North Oregon Street
P.O. Box 1891
Jacksonville, OR 97530
Phone (541) 899-8938
Toll Free (800) 846-8422
Fax (541) 899-3992
E-mail: touvelle@wave.net
Website: http://www.wave.net/upg/touvelle

Rates:
High Season: $80 - 155 U.S.
Low Season: $70 - 135 U.S.

Touvelle House

Jacksonville, Oregon sprouted in the wake of gold rush fever, which began in 1852 after a prospector found paydirt in nearby Rich Gulch Creek. Those who rushed to the foothills of the Siskiyous to seek their fortunes also found agricultural riches. The fertile soil and temperate climate of the Rogue Valley was ideal for farming. Jacksonville became a hub of commerce and the county seat. The action continued for several decades until the gold veins ran dry and the newfangled railroad arrived across the valley, in Medford, drawing trade and government with it.

Agriculture continued to be a source of income for many settlers, however, and Jacksonville became known for its orchards. Frank Touvelle, of Blosser, Ohio, had heard of the wonderful climate in "the Italy of Oregon" and decided to head west with his bride, Elizabeth to seek their fortune.

The Touvelles purchased a small house, and a few orchards upon their arrival. As their business prospered, the Touvelles decided to build a new house, incorporating their original home into the structure. The result was a stately Craftsman-style residence, which today welcomes visitors as Touvelle House Bed and Breakfast.

Acquiring Touvelle House, Dennis and Carolee Casey realized a longtime dream of restoring an old home to its period style and opening it as a bed and breakfast. The Caseys recently hired Don and Susan Riehlman to run the inn, and it hums along in their capable hands.

The house sits on a generous acre and is framed by two enormous old oak trees, looking appropriately old-fashioned in its setting. A broad staircase ushers guests onto the veranda and into the wood-paneled lobby. The main floor is the common area and offers guests plenty of room to roam. A beautifully furnished formal Great Room evokes turn of the century elegance. French doors lead into the dining room which features a handsome built in buffet, a classic feature of Craftsman architecture. A small library is the gathering place for readers and those who wish to watch television. The charming sunroom is being transformed into a gift shop with handcrafted jewelry, cards, jams and jellies from local artists and craftspeople.

There are six rooms at Touvelle House, spread over three floors. The sole room on the main floor is the Judge's Chambers, named in honor of Mr. Touvelle, which is located just off the Great Room and ideal for the single traveler. Many guests favor the second floor Americana Room with its burgundy, blue and white decor. A patchwork quilt sets the tone for this tastefully patriotic choice. The Forest Glade is handsomely decorated with dark walnut armoire and bed, and a decorative fireplace adds character. The Garden Suite can accommodate up to four guests in floral pastel comfort. On the third floor, the Prairie Room's furnishings are reminiscent of Jacksonville's pioneer days. Granny's Attic is cozy with floral wallpaper, patchwork quilt and a snug reading corner with sofa and rustic pine chest.

While the decor may be old-fashioned, the amenities are very current. All rooms have their own telephone plus an additional jack for laptops. Business travelers are welcomed here, with corporate rates during the week, and accommodations for small meetings. The summer heat is intense so the air-conditioning and outdoor pool are refreshing features of the inn. Additional touches include fresh flowers in rooms and turn-down service with chocolate truffles.

Guests can walk the two blocks into Jacksonville and the quaint town still looks as though a stagecoach might come rumbling around the corner any minute. Many buildings in the historic downtown area have been restored and Jacksonville is designated as an Historic Landmark District. Its period look has attracted Hollywood and California Street has been featured in several films. Collectors can browse the many antique shops while others may enjoy the Jacksonville Museum which highlights the history of the Rogue Valley. Those curious about former residents may find some interest in the Jacksonville Cemetery.

One former resident, Peter Britt, a famous photographer and horticulturist, is now known by the outdoor music and arts festival that takes place on the grounds of his onetime home. The Britt Festival runs June through September in Jacksonville and draws a mix of performers, including dance, musical theater, jazz, bluegrass, folk and country. Some big names perform, too, and avid music lovers can picnic while enjoying their favorite stars under the night sky.

The kitchen at Touvelle House will prepare Britt Baskets upon request which might include the delectable peanut butter "house cookies" baked daily. Dessert lovers will find Touvelle House breakfasts a real treat as the meal often closes with a sweet. Tangy lemon tart, warm gingerbread, raspberry trifle or fruit crisp are just a few choices. Other menu items might include French toast, either stuffed or with a streusel topping, or a savory breakfast casserole of eggs, bacon and cheddar cheese. Fruit smoothies are a popular beginning to the meal.

After breakfast, guests can retire to one of three verandas to plan their days activities or sip one last cup of coffee while admiring the well-manicured grounds.

Touvelle House Breakfast Casserole

Serves 6-8

1	pkg. hash brown patties
3	oz. cream cheese
1	cup sour cream
1-1/2	cups grated cheddar cheese
4	eggs
1/2	cup chopped bell pepper
1/2	cup chopped onion
1/2	cup sliced mushrooms
1/2	cup sliced zucchini
1	lb. bacon, cooked and crumbled
	salt and pepper

Preheat oven to 350° F. Grease a 9" x 13" pan.

Mix together cream cheese, sour cream, 1/2 cup cheddar cheese and eggs. Add salt and pepper to taste.

Place hash brown patties in pan, season well with salt and pepper. Pour egg mixture over patties. Top with chopped vegetables, cover with foil and bake for 55 minutes.

Remove foil, add cooked, crumbled bacon and remaining 1 cup grated cheddar cheese. Bake for an additional 10 minutes, uncovered, or until cheese is melted and bubbling.

Remove from oven, let cool several minutes, then cut into squares for serving.

There is no love sincerer than the love of food.

George Bernard Shaw

It was obvious that the egg had come first.
There was something dignified about a silent, passive egg,
whereas Aunt Irene found it difficult to envision an angel
bearing a hen – which despite its undoubted merits,
was a foolish and largely intractable bird.

Alice Thomas Ellis

Tyee Lodge

4925 NW Woody Way
Newport, OR 97365
Phone (541) 265-8953
Toll Free (888) 553-8933
Email: mcconn@teleport.com
Website: www.newportnet.com/tyee/home.htm

Rates: $85 - 120 U.S.

Tyee Lodge

The spectacular shoreline of Oregon's Pacific coast stretches 400 miles from Brookings, near the California border, to Astoria at the mouth of the Columbia River. Natural wonders and spectacular sights inspire awe all along the way. Just north of Newport stands one such wonder. The Yaquina Head Outstanding Natural Area juts out into the Pacific Ocean, offering dramatic views, several hiking trails and tide pools for exploring. Home to Yaquina Head Lighthouse, one of the first navigational aids on the coast, and the Yaquina Head Interpretive Center, this area presents a close-up of marine life and a lesson in natural history.

The natural beauty of the area inspired Mark and Cindy McConnell to create a retreat that celebrated this splendor. Their inn, which Mark calls a modern-day lodge, is perched on a bluff overlooking Agate Beach. Yaquina Head is within view to the north. Newport has been a resort destination for over a century. It's popularity is evident in the heavy stream of cars up and down Highway 101. Tyee Lodge is situated well off the busy thoroughfare, and north of town. Pounding waves, wind in the trees and seabirds are the only traffic here.

The bright white living room is comfy with Craftsman-style tables, oversized plaid sofas and chairs, along with the requisite fireplace. Wood-trimmed windows create simple frames for the dramatic seascapes outside. Guests can curl up here and watch waves crash on the beach below or enjoy similar dramatic views from their rooms.

When the 40s era home was remodeled by the McConnels, the guest quarters were rewarded with private baths, but more importantly, with well-placed windows that are the focal point of each space. Room monikers reflect the oceanside location and its inhabitants; Salmon (with its own fireplace), Lighthouse, Oregon Natives, Coastal Rainforest and Shorebirds. Well-chosen wall hangings and accessories underscore each theme. Golden pine furnishings and fluffy down comforters add to the lodge-y feel.

Wilford Brimley could film a Quaker Oats ad in the dining room. Seated in wood-backed chairs, guests gather around the large oak table for family-style dining. The fare leans towards the healthy with Northwest flair. The McConnels strive to keep menus low in fat and cholesterol, although the traditional breakfast treats are within reach for those so inclined. Fruit begins the meal - fruit parfaits, baked apples, or a warm spiced fruit compote in winter. Whole wheat orange pancakes or a thick vegetable frittata provide sustenance for long walks on the beach. Gooey cinnamon rolls or fresh-from-the-oven coffeecake, crisp roasted potatoes and juicy sausages are amongst the temptations available for greater appetites

A complimentary beverage bar quenches thirst throughout the day. Freshly brewed coffee joins a pot of hot water ready to steep a teabag or create instant cocoa and cider. The small refrigerator holds wine and sodas. Guests are welcome to stash their own snacks inside. A rainy day at the ocean might call for munching popcorn by the fire – a microwave stands at the ready to pop bags of "light" kernels thoughtfully provided by the health-conscious McConnels.

Settle into an Adirondack chair outside and admire the perennial beds bordering the grounds. Protected from the north winds in the summer, this is the perfect spot for soaking up some rays while admiring the scenery through the pines. The cliffside location is also ideal for watching the sun set into the ocean, kept toasty by the flames in the outdoor fire pit. Pull out the fleece jacket and put on those favorite boots to hike down the trail to the beach. Comb the beach, collect some driftwood and spy on all the activity going on in those tide pools. Lucky observers can see whales pass on their twice yearly migratory travels.

Tyee Quiche

Serves 6-8

This recipe is named in honor of the mighty chinook salmon, known as tyee in Chinook jargon. The crustless quiche is quick and easy to make. The recipe can be prepared in one pan to serve a group or in custard cups for individual servings.

4	eggs
1/4	cup butter, melted
1/2	cup buttermilk baking mix
1-1/2	cups skim milk
1	cup grated cheese (use cheddar, swiss, monterey jack, parmesan or a combination)
3/4	cup smoked salmon, flaked or chopped

Preheat oven to 350° F. Spray a 9" pie or quiche pan with vegetable spray.

Beat together eggs, baking mix, and melted butter. Mixture will be slightly lumpy. Add milk and stir to blend.

Pour egg mixture into prepared pan, sprinkle with the salmon and grated cheese, pressing them down into egg mixture.

Bake for 45 minutes or until golden brown and set. If using small souffle dishes or custard cups for individual servings, bake for approximately 20 minutes.

Remove from oven, let rest for a minute or two, then cut into wedges to serve.

Cinnamon Roll Rose

Makes 2 - 9" diameter rings, serving 12-16

The dough created from this recipe is stored in the refrigerator until ready to use. It can be formed into rings, as called for in this version, or cut into individual rolls.

1	cup milk, scalded
1/4	cup butter
1/4	cup sugar
1	egg
3-1/2 -4	cups flour
1/4	cup lukewarm water
1	pkg. active dry yeast (2 1/4 tsp.)

Scald the milk in a saucepan over medium heat until small bubbles appear at the outer edge. Add butter and stir to melt. Milk and butter can also be scalded together in the microwave for two minutes.

Pour milk mixture into a large bowl. Add sugar and egg and mix well. Add 2 cups of flour, mixing well. By now the dough should be lukewarm. If not, let it cool a bit.

Combine the lukewarm water and yeast, and let yeast dissolve. Add yeast to the dough and stir in well.

Add the remaining flour, using just enough to create a soft dough, and knead for about one minute. Transfer the dough to a buttered or greased bowl and turn the dough in the bowl to coat the surface.

Cover with plastic wrap and refrigerate for at least two hours or up to five days.

Continued on next page

Making the rolls

Plan to assemble the roll two to two and a half hours prior to serving.

- 1/4 cup butter, melted
- 1 Tbs. cinnamon
- 1/2 cup brown sugar
- 1 cup raisins or currants, if desired

Spray two 9" round pans with vegetable spray. Remove d(refrigerator and divide in half. Set aside one half and roll out half on a floured board until about 1/4" thick and twice as lo

Brush dough with half the butter, and sprinkle with half mon, half the brown sugar and half the raisins, if desired. R up from the long side, and seal seam. Transfer roll to pan a(ring. Using scissors, snip through the roll across the top, e٠ inches or so, keeping the bottom of the roll uncut. Turn each partially cut roll to the side of the pan, forming a rose pattern.

Repeat the above steps with remaining dough.

Let rise for 1-2 hours in a warm place or, heat the oven to 200° F., turn it off and place rolls inside with the door open until they double.

Bake rolls in a 375° F. oven for 10-12 minutes or until golden. Let cool slightly and transfer to serving platter. Serve while warm. If desired, rolls may be glazed with the following:

Powdered Sugar Icing

- 1 cup sifted powdered sugar
- 1/4 tsp. vanilla
- milk or orange juice

Mix powdered sugar and vanilla and 1 tablespoon milk or juice and stir together. Add additional milk or juice 1 teaspoon at a time until desired consistency is reached. Drizzle over rolls while still warm.

Washington Bed & Breakfast Inns

Amy's Manor
Ann Starrett Mansion
Captain Whidbey Inn
Chambered Nautilus
Channel House
Chestnut Hill Inn
Colonel Crockett Farm
Groveland Cottage
James House
Lake Union Bed & Breakfast
Olympic Lights
Purple House
Schnauzer Crossing
Shelburne Inn
Turtleback Farm Inn
Waverly Place Bed & Breakfast

I had an excellent repast – the best possible –
which consisted simply of boiled eggs and bread and butter.
It was the quality of these ingredients that made the occasion
memorable. The eggs were so good that I am ashamed to say
how many of them I consumed. It might seem that an egg
which has succeeded in being fresh has done all that
can reasonably be expected of it.

Henry James

Amy's Manor
Bed and Breakfast

435 Highway 153
Pateros, WA 98846
Phone (509) 923-2334
Fax (509) 923-2691
Website: http://www.amysmanor.com

Rates: $80 U.S.

Amy's Manor Bed & Breakfast

Pamela Miller's grandparents homesteaded in the Methow Valley and their residence, built in 1928, is now a bed and breakfast named for Pam's grandmother, Amy. Stucco-faced and green shuttered, the house is surrounded by stone fences, looking properly English in this very western backdrop. The inn sits on 170 acres of farmland between the Cascade foothills and the Methow River in the heart of this apple-growing valley.

Pam trained at the Culinary Institute of America and cooked in the Bay Area and at Seattle's well-known Fullers Restaurant. Taking some time off to ponder a permanent move to the Bay Area, Pam returned to Pateros for a vacation and ended up staying on a permanent basis. In addition to running the inn and doing all of the cooking, Pam also teaches cooking and gardening classes.

The organic vegetable garden is a lesson in itself, best learned at the dining table. Menus are centered around what's ripe in the garden. Farm fresh eggs, lemon or oatmeal buttermilk pancakes, flavorful bacon and sausages from the butcher in Twisp and a profusion of vegetables from the garden are woven into tasty meals partnered by freshly pressed apple cider from the orchard and Pam's homebaked breads and muffins. Friday and Saturday the inn is open for dinner to outside guests and Pam cooks up three to four course meals for up to 23 in her elegant dining room. A meal here is reputed to be the one of the finest to be found in the Valley.

Three fortunate parties in the dining room will be lucky enough to have booked a room at the inn. Each space has a view of the Methow River and flower gardens and offers generous queen beds. Country French in decor, the rooms are filled with a collection of antiques and handmade quilts. Two baths service all three rooms, and plans are in the works to add a third.

A leisurely atmosphere exists at the inn, and guests are encouraged to relax and enjoy the solitude. Bring a book or knitting, for there is no television here. Anyone who can't sit still will find plenty to keep busy. Springtime brings river rafting season, followed by summer hikes and mountain biking. Winter sports include cross-country skiing, snow-mobiling and snow-shoeing. Day trippers can cruise north on Highway 153, paralleling the Methow River, and visit tiny Twisp, western-themed Winthrop and scout the controversial Early Winters development in Mazama. A southbound trip on the same highway will bring travelers to the town of Chelan, sitting at southern tip of popular Lake Chelan, a favorite destination for water sports and spectacular scenery.

Pears Simmered in Cider

Serves 4

Bosc pears grow in the orchards at Amy's Manor and are perfect for the start of a hearty fall breakfast. While the pears simmer, the cook can continue with other breakfast preparations. The Bosc is also very forgiving to work with as it won't get mushy if not served right away.

2	firm Bosc pears
3	cups raw, unpasteurized apple cider
1/2	cup sugar
1/4	tsp. nutmeg
1/2	tsp. ginger
1/4	tsp. cinnamon
1/4	tsp. allspice
1	cinnamon stick
1/4	cup dried cranberries
	crème fraiche, optional (see recipe below)

Continued on next page

Preheat oven to 250° F. and place four serving plates inside to warm. Put the apple cider and sugar in an 8" sauté pan and bring to a boil. Turn down to a simmer and add all the spices.

Peel the pears and cut in half lengthwise, removing the core with a melon baller or metal teaspoon. Place the pears in the cider, turn once to coat and then simmer, cut side down for 15 minutes. Add the dried cranberries and then turn the pears over to cook on the other side, about 10 minutes more. Pears are done when a knife slides into the core area. If the syrup does not coat the back of a spoon, and pears are done, remove the pears and reduce syrup to desired consistency.

To serve pears, remove serving plates from oven, slice each pear from just below stem end to base, about 3/8" thick, being careful not to sever fruit from stem end. Using a spatula, transfer pears to serving plate and press lightly to fan slices.

Spoon cranberries and syrup over fanned pears and garnish with a cinnamon stick. A dollop of crème fraiche can be added if desired. Grate nutmeg over crème fraiche to garnish.

Crème Fraiche
- 1 cup heavy cream
- 1 cup sour cream

In a ceramic bowl, combine the cream and sour cream. Cover and let sit at room temperature for 24 hours. When it has thickened, refrigerate until ready to use.

Ann Starrett Mansion

744 Clay Street
Port Townsend, WA 98368
Phone (360) 385-3205
Toll Free (800) 321-0644
Fax (360) 385-2976

Rates: $85 - 115 U.S.

THE GOURMET'S GUIDE TO NORTHWEST BED & BREAKFAST INNS

Ann Starrett Mansion

Designated as a national historic landmark, Port Townsend, Washington is a treasure trove of Victorian architecture. One of the most elaborate examples of this era is the unique and fanciful Ann Starrett Mansion, built as a wedding gift to Mrs. Starrett from her wealthy contractor husband, George.

Mr. Starrett spared no expense when building this tribute to his bride. The focal point of the exterior is the four-storied tower crowned with a circle of tiny, gabled windows. Inside the tower is one of the most capricious features of the home - an eight-sided domed ceiling, each panel depicting one of the Four Seasons alternated with the Four Virtues. To honor his bride, George Starrett had the artist paint each graceful figure to resemble his beloved Ann. The tiny windows in the tower hold ruby glass, through which, on the first day of each season, a ray of red light glows on the corresponding panel.

The frescoed ceiling can be viewed standing in the entry or more closely inspected by climbing the freestanding staircase which encircles the inside of the tower to the third floor with no visible means of support. Its fabrication remains a mystery. Mr. Starrett hired an itinerant worker to build it, who in turn sealed off the home during the staircases' construction. An offer to tear down the staircase and discover its magical underpinnings, then rebuild it, has thus far been rebuffed by owners Bob and Edel Sokol.

WASHINGTON BED & BREAKFAST INNS

The Sokols have devoted as much love to restoring the Starrett mansion as the original occupants did building it. The home had passed through a series of owners, and been empty for three years, when the Sokols purchased it in 1986. Giving themselves five years to restore the house and create a viable business, the Sokols set to work.

A new roof was added. Layers of unattractive wallpaper were stripped when it was discovered, via descendant Virginia Starrett, that Ann had not originally papered the walls. Then came paint - robin's egg blue in one of the parlors to match the frescoes uncovered by a previous owner. Mauve, plum, shell pink and pale green in guest rooms. Mustard yellow warmed the dining room. The legendary solar calendar frescoes were restored and enough bathrooms added to satisfy modern demands.

Then it was time to furnish the mansion. Two truckloads of antiques, brought by the Sokols from the Midwest, were carefully displayed throughout the rooms. Finding this not enough, the Sokols continued to purchase pieces to create the comfortably jammed interiors so loved by the Victorians. Happily, some of the Starrett's possessions were in the hands of local dealers and these cherished items are now home again, thanks to Edel.

Inspired by the elaborate sets of old films, Edel has added some unusual touches. In one of the guest baths, the exterior of the tub is painted with whimsical cherubs and vines, similar to one she'd seen in a John Wayne movie. Told by guests that four poster beds were romantic, Edel installed a Renaissance version in one of the guest rooms, enclosing the red velvet-covered bed and its tall headboard with floor to ceiling draperies. If ever there was a bed to spur the imagination, this is it.

Guest rooms occupy four floors of the mansion, from the attic where the Sokols lived upon moving in, to the brick walled Garden Suite on the carriage house level, where Ann Starrett was dropped off by her carriage driver. Two additional rooms can be found in Starrett Cottage, which was added in the '30s. The upper room is decorated in a Far East motif, a tribute to some of Port Townsend's trading partners from the last century. The lower room offers the modern addition of a Jacuzzi tub and both rooms are accented by river rock gas fireplaces.

The fireplace in the main parlor was added, surprisingly, in 1968. When the house was built in 1899, central heating was installed. By excluding fireplaces, George Starrett made a statement of his wealth and modernity. The handsome mantel now displayed was rescued from a Chicago mansion awaiting demolition. A ribbon of elaborate, neo-classically inspired frieze rims the room. The hand-stenciled frieze decorating the ceiling is the handiwork of a traveling artist from San Francisco who commented that "having an unpainted ceiling was like having an earth without a sky". Such whimsy is the trademark of Ann Starrett Mansion.

Rose Petal Jam

This lovely delicacy works well on thinly sliced white bread spread with sweet butter. Be sure to use pesticide-free rose petals.

- 1/2 lb. dark rose petals
- 1 lb. sugar
- 5 cups purified water
- juice of 2 lemons

Snip the white triangles from the rose petal bases, then tear the petals to fine shreds. Sprinkle them with enough sugar from the main quantity to cover, and leave overnight. This intensifies the fragrance and darkens the crimson of the petals.

Prepare 4 half-pint canning jars according to manufacturer's instructions. Dissolve the remaining sugar in the water and lemon juice over low heat. Stir in the sugared rose petals and simmer for 20 minutes. Then bring to a boil, and boil for 5 minutes until mixture thickens. (This jam is not brought to setting point, so disregard the usual tests.)

Transfer jam to glass jars, seal and store in refrigerator. Makes about 4 cups jam.

> She sent for one of those short, plump little cakes
> called "petite madeleines," which look as though they had been
> molded in the fluted scallop of the pilgrim's shell.
> And soon, mechanically, weary after a dull day with the prospect
> of a depressing morrow, I raised to my lips a spoonful of cake.
> A shudder ran through my whole body and I stopped,
> intent upon the extraordinary changes that were taking place.
>
> *Marcel Proust*
> Remembrance of Things Past

Madeleines

This recipe makes about a dozen of the little French sponge cakes made famous by Proust. Traditionally baked in tins of long, shell-shaped molds, madeleines can also be made in shallow tart plaques, though this may rob the diner of some romance. For ultimate enjoyment, serve madeleines with tilleul (lime blossom) tea, which is thought to enhance the light lemon flavor of the cakes.

- 2 eggs, separated
- 1/2 cup sugar
- 1/2 cup butter, melted
- grated rind and juice of 1/2 lemon
- 1/2 cup self-rising flour

Preheat oven to 350° F. Lightly butter madeleine or tart tins.

Beat the egg yolks and sugar until thoroughly mixed but still bright yellow. Beat in melted butter, lemon rind and juice, then sift flour over surface and fold in. Beat egg white with a fork until foamy, then beat them into the batter well.

Spoon a small amount of batter into each mold and bake in the center of the oven for 20 minutes. Cool slightly in the molds before gently easing out onto wire racks to complete cooling.

These are best eaten fresh.

In the light of what Proust wrote with so mild a stimulus,
it is the world's loss that he did not have a heartier appetite.
On a dozen Gardiner's Island oysters, a bowl of clam chowder,
a peck of steamers, some bay scallops, three sauteed soft-shelled crabs,
a few ears of fresh-picked corn, a thin swordfish steak of generous area,
a pair of lobsters, and a piece of Long Island duck,
he might have written a masterpiece.

A. J. Liebling

Madeira Cake

Serves 8

In the Victorian era, this simple cake was traditionally served mid-morning with a glass of Madeira, thus earning its name.

- 3/4 cup butter
- 3/4 cup sugar
- 1 Tbs. ground almonds
- 3 eggs, beaten
- 1-1/2 cups self-rising flour
- grated peel of 1-1/2 lemons
- 2 large strips of candied citron

Preheat oven to 375° F. Grease an 8" cake pan and line bottom with a round of wax or parchment paper.

Cream together butter and sugar until light and fluffy. Sprinkle in ground almonds and stir until incorporated. Add the eggs, a little at a time, beating well after each addition. Fold in the flour and grated lemon zest.

Transfer mixture into prepared pan and bake for one hour. Open oven door, carefully slide out rack and place two citron strips crisscross on dome of cake. Bake for an additional 30 minutes.

Cool cake in pan for several minutes, then turn out on a wire rack to complete cooling.

Bourbon does for me
what the piece of cake did for Proust.

Walker Percy

The Captain Whidbey Inn

2072 West Captain Whidbey Inn Road
Coupeville, WA 98239
Phone (360) 678-4097
Toll Free (800) 366-4097
Fax 360/678-4110
E-Mail: captain@whidbey.net
Website: http://www.captainwhidbey.com

Rates: $95 - 205 U.S.

The Captain Whidbey Inn

A visit to the Captain Whidbey Inn means, in all likelihood, a close encounter of the crustacean kind – with mytulis edulis, of course, the black, jewel-like mussels which are the treasure of the Island's celebrated Penn Cove. The Inn devotes the first weekend in March to celebrating the shellfish at the Mussel Festival, where revelers can indulge in recipe and eating contests, cooking demos, a mussel "chowder off", as well as wine and beer tastings paired with complementary menus designed by Executive Chef Sam Chapman

The Inn's prix fixe dinner menu changes with the seasons, but always features the mussel, succulent and tender whether bathed in white wine sweetened with butter and fresh basil, or glistening in a broth of sake, sesame oil, garlic and ginger. Winter months might feature pine nut-crusted Alaskan rockfish crowned with nasturtuim butter and summer, alder-planked salmon with molasses apple cider glaze.

In warm weather, the outdoor fire pit is used to bake the planked salmon in a traditional style reminiscent of local Natives. Just a glowing ember's throw distant lies the Inn's herb garden. Lovingly tended by a full-time gardener, the neatly laid paths and well-marked plants offer a quick primer of menu ingredients. Chef Chapman utilizes the wealth of the garden in his cooking whenever possible.

Overnight guests can savor breakfast entrees of honey whole wheat pancakes with blueberry ketchup and mint butter, Captain Whidbey's housemade granola, fresh fruits and Chef Chapman's rosemary popovers, crumpets and lemon poppyseed bread, warm from the oven, offered with local berry jams and apple butter from orchards on the grounds.

The rustic Inn was built in 1907 and is now designated as a National Landmark. A log cabin feel is reinfored by the inn's lobby which sports an enormous stone fireplace and comfortable sofas warmed by the glow of the exposed log walls. Upstairs, the inn's cozy rooms beckon with feather beds and down comforters. Guests share bathrooms, located down the hallway, or opt instead for private cabins overlooking Penn Cove, cottages with full kitchens or rooms with a lagoon view.

While waiting for dinner to be served, charter the classic ketch Cutty Sark for a tour of the Cove and mussel farm, play a round of golf, go kayaking, or simply relax on the spacious deck. Don't miss the quaint bar festooned with marine paraphernalia and empty bottles, mementos which stand as testament to festivities past.

Spiced Fruit Compote

Yield: 1 quart

- 1 cup golden raisins
- 1 cup dried apricots, sliced in half
- 1 cup prunes
- 1 cup dried peaches
- 2-1/2 cups water
- 1/4 cup sugar
- 1/2 cup port wine
- 1 tsp. vanilla extract

Bouquet garni of:

- 1 cinnamon stick
- 4 whole cloves
- 1/4" slice fresh ginger.

Wrap the cinnamon, cloves and ginger in a small square of cheesecloth and tie corners together with kitchen twine

Combine fruits together in a mixing bowl and set aside.

In a medium saucepan, mix together water, sugar, port wine, vanilla and bouquet garni. Bring to a boil over medium heat, cooking until sugar dissolves. Remove from heat.

Add fruits to saucepan and let sit in poaching liquid until poaching liquid is no longer hot. Remove bouquet garni and serve compote warm. The compote can be chilled and reheated.

The Captain Whidbey Inn Lemon Poppy Seed Bread

Yield: 2 loaves

Bread

- 1 cup butter
- 2 cups sugar
- 4 eggs
- 3 cups flour
- 2 tsp. baking powder
- 1 tsp. salt
- 1 cup milk
- zest of 2 lemons (save lemons for glaze)
- 1/4 cup poppy seeds

Glaze

- Juice of 2 lemons
- 1 cup sugar

Whisk together until sugar is dissolved

Preheat oven to 350° F. and prepare two - 8" x 4" x 3" loaf pans by brushing with melted butter and dusting with flour

Cream together butter and sugar, add eggs and mix well. Sift dry ingredients together, mix in poppy seeds and add to butter mixture.

Add grated lemon zest to milk in a separate bowl. Add milk to the batter, mixing until dry ingredients are incorporated. Do not overmix.

Transfer batter to prepared loaf pans and bake for one hour.

Remove bread from oven and let cool. Remove bread from pans and brush with two coats of lemon glaze.

The Captain Whidbey Inn Crab Cakes

Yield: 2 dozen 2-inch cakes

Use fresh Dungeness crab for the best flavor.

Crab Cakes
- 2 eggs
- 1/2 cup mayonnaise
- 1/2 tsp. dry mustard
- 1/2 tsp. red pepper (cayenne)
- 1/2 tsp. Tabasco
- 1/2 tsp. salt
- 1/2 tsp. white pepper
- 1-1/4 lb. cooked crab meat, picked over for shells
- 1/4 cup chopped parsley
- 4 Tbs. capers
- 6 Tbs. diced roasted red peppers (pimiento)
- 2 cups fine bread crumbs
- 2 tsp. Pernod

Coating/Breading
- 2 cups flour
- 2 cups cornmeal

Beat eggs in medium mixing bowl. Add mayo, spices, salt, white pepper and Tabasco; mix until smooth. Add crab meat. Mix in parsley, capers, red pepper, bread crumbs and Pernod. Taste and correct seasoning if desired.

Spread breading mix on a cookie sheet. Using an ice cream scoop for portioning pat and shape crab cakes. Dredge cakes in breading mix and transfer to a baking sheet.

Heat over medium enough olive oil to cover a medium skillet. Add crab cakes and cook until golden, about 3 minutes per side. Keep warm in a 300° F. oven while cooking remaining cakes.

The Captain Whidbey Inn Granola

Yield: 4 pounds

4	oz. sliced almonds
4	oz. pecans
8	oz . sunflower seeds
3/4	cup vegetable oil
2	Tbs. sesame seed oil
1/4	tsp. salt
4	Tbs. vanilla
1/2	cup honey
1/2	cup molasses
1-3/4	lb. rolled oats
1/4	cup sesame seeds
8	oz. raisins

Preheat oven to 350° F. Place almonds, pecans and sunflower seeds on a cookie sheet and toast until golden. Watch carefully as nuts burn easily. Combine oils, salt, vanilla, honey and molasses in a medium saucepan and heat to consistency of oil. Place oats and sesame seeds in mixing bowl and pour over warm oil mixture and stir until oat, seed & oil mixture are well-mixed. Transfer oat mixture to a roasting pan and bake for 1 hour, stirring mixture every 15 minutes. Remove from oven and stir in raisins and toasted nuts. Cool and store in plastic bags or containers

The Chambered Nautilus

5005 22nd Avenue N.E.
Seattle, WA 98105
Phone (206) 522-2536
Toll Free (800) 545-8459
Fax (206) 528-0898
E-mail: Chamberednautilus@msn.com

Rates: $89 - 119 U.S.

The Chambered Nautilus

According the to the American Heritage Dictionary, a nautilus is "a cephalopod mollusk of the genus Nautilus, found in the Indian and Pacific oceans and having a spiral, pearly-lined shell with a series of air-filled chambers. Also called "chambered nautilus." The air-filled chambers of the nautilus provide a haven for sea creatures.

In a similar fashion, the chambers of this bed and breakfast nautilus provide a haven for world-weary bipeds. This particular shell was built in the Georgian colonial style and its six rooms, while not pearly-lined, offer an array of nature-based decorative themes in which to relax.

The former home of the first professor of Oriental Studies at the University of Washington, Dr. Gowen, the Chambered Nautilus sits tucked on a hillside, resting comfortably above the street. Climbing the stairs, the scent of daphne wafts down, instantly welcoming and relaxing. A candy-apple red door greets guests as they arrive. The lavender-hued entry beckons while homemade chocolate butterscotch oatmeal cookies and aromatic coffee await in the pale green living room.

A bright, white sun porch overlooks the garden and offers an ideal breakfast spot or idyllic respite for reading. The rosy dining room features a fireplace perfect for cozy winter dining. Menu items might feature rosemary (innkeeper Steve Poole's favorite culinary herb) mint or chives. An herb garden is being fashioned while the grounds are being re-landscaped to provide more botanical ingredients and inspire new recipes.

The Inn's proximity to the University offers a multitude of cultural activities. Two newly remodeled museums, The Burke Museum and the Henry Art Gallery are within walking distance. Meany Theatre features a variety of programs; dance, music and live theater. A few steps further to "The Ave" as University Way is known, and cultural quests give way to more prosaic pastimes such as ethnic dining and people-watching.

WASHINGTON BED & BREAKFAST INNS

Filmgoers take note! Several small independents show first-run films, foreign features and older classics on their screens.

If those barking dogs still have some bow-wow left, a bike trip on the Burke-Gilman Trail might be just the ticket! The Trail is a brief walk from the Inn and a bike rental shop is nearby. Or hop in your auto and head to the Waterfront Activities Center and rent a canoe for an urban paddle on Lake Washington, underneath the 520 bridge and into the lily padded, muffled world of green on the shores of the Washington Park Arboretum. The Arboretum is a destination in itself, an in-city wooded parkland including a stunning Japanese Tea Garden. If shopping is your passion, then the newly rejuvenated University Village should satisfy just about any retail craving.

After all the activity, no doubt some food will be needed to sustain further pursuits. Steve and his wife, Joyce Schulte, happily provide suggestions for neighborhood restaurants and those farther afield. Anything from a quick snack to a full evening's dining is available nearby. When the repast is past, it's time to return to that safe haven for land creatures, the Chambered Nautilus.

———⟫•◇•⟪———

If you accept a dinner invitation,
you have a moral obligation to be amusing.

Wallis, Duchess of Windsor

Rosemary Buttermilk Muffins

Yield: 12 muffins

Innkeeper Steve Poole recommends that these muffins be enjoyed warm from the oven, when their flavor is best.

- 2 cups unbleached all-purpose flour
- 2 Tbs. granulated sugar
- 4 tsp. baking powder
- 1/2 tsp. baking soda
- 1/2 tsp. salt
- 1/2 tsp. onion powder
- 1 tsp. dried rosemary
- 1/2 cup vegetable shortening, melted
- 1 cup buttermilk
- 2 Tbs. grated parmesan cheese

Position rack in center of oven and preheat to 400° F. Grease muffin pan.

In a 2-1/2 quart mixing bowl, sift together flour, sugar, baking powder, salt, soda and onion powder. Crush rosemary and add to sifted ingredients, stirring to blend.

In a 1-1/2 quart mixing bowl, whisk melted shortening with buttermilk; beat thoroughly.

Make a well in the center of the dry ingredients, pour buttermilk mixture into well and stir together only until flour is moistened.

Spoon into prepared tins and sprinkle with grated parmesan.

Bake for 15 minutes or until golden brown. Cool for several minutes before turning onto wire rack. Serve warm.

Northwest Salmon Breakfast Pie

Serves 6

This recipe is an excellent way to enjoy leftover salmon. Cooked shrimp or crab can be substituted for the salmon, or use a combination of the three.

1	8-inch prepared pie crust
3	Tbs. butter
1	cup chopped onion (about 1 large onion)
1	clove garlic, minced
12	oz. fully cooked salmon, flaked and de-boned
5	eggs, beaten
2-1/4	cups dairy sour cream
1/4	cup all-purpose flour
1-1/2	cups shredded Swiss cheese
1	tsp. dill weed

Preheat oven to 400° F. Bake pie shell for 8 minutes and remove from oven. Reduce oven temperature to 375° F.

Melt butter in a saute pan. When butter is foaming, add onion and garlic. Saute until onion is translucent, but not golden.

In a medium bowl, combine eggs, sour cream and flour. Add flaked and de-boned salmon and the onion mixture to the eggs. Stir in 1 cup of grated Swiss and dill.

Pour filling into partially baked shell. Sprinkle with remaining cheese. Bake at 375° F. for 40-45 minutes. Cover with foil during the final 15 minutes of baking to prevent over browning. Remove from oven and cool for 5 minutes before serving.

Pumpkin Spice Bread

Makes 3 medium loaves

This bread is a snap to make and freezes well, too.

3	cups flour
3-1/2	cups sugar
1-1/2	tsp. cinnamon
1-1/2	tsp. nutmeg
1-1/2	tsp. salt
2	tsp. baking soda
1	cup corn oil
2/3	cup water
4	eggs
1	can pumpkin, 14 oz.
1-1/2	cups chopped walnuts, optional
1	cup raisins, optional

Preheat oven to 350° F. Grease three 8" x 5" x 3" loaf pans.

In a large bowl, mix together flour, sugar, spices, salt and soda. Add the oil, water, eggs and pumpkin, mixing well. Stir in nuts and raisins, if desired.

Divide batter equally between loaf pans. Bake at 350° F. for one hour or until knife inserted in center of the loaf comes out clean. Turn out onto wire racks to cool.

Marmalade-Stuffed French Toast with Orange Syrup

Serves 4

8	2-1/4 by 4-1/2-inch slices French bread, each about 1 inch thick
4	oz. cream cheese, at room temperature
1/4	cup orange marmalade
4	large eggs
1	cup milk
1	tsp. vanilla extract
1/4	tsp. ground cinnamon
1/8	tsp. nutmeg
2	Tbs. butter
	Orange Syrup (recipe follows)

Preheat oven to 300° F. Place baking sheet in oven.

Cutting through top crust of each bread slice, make 4-inch long by 2-inch deep pocket.

Stir together cream cheese and marmalade in small bowl. Spoon 1 generous tablespoonful of cream cheese mixture into each pocket.

Whisk together eggs, milk, vanilla, cinnamon and nutmeg in pie plate. Dip 4 stuffed bread slices into egg mixture, coating completely.

Melt 1 tablespoon butter in large nonstick skillet over medium heat. Add dipped bread to skillet. Cook until golden brown, about 2 minutes per side.

Transfer French toast to baking sheet in oven. Repeat dipping and cooking with remaining 4 bread slices, egg mixture and 1 tablespoon butter.

Continued on next page

Orange Syrup

    3/4   cup frozen orange juice concentrate
    1/2   cup butter (1 stick)
    1/2   cup sugar

Combine orange juice concentrate, butter and sugar in small saucepan. Stir over low heat until butter melts and sugar dissolves — do not boil!

Remove from heat. Cool slightly. Syrup can be made 2 days ahead. Keep refrigerated and re-warm over low heat.

Channel House

2902 Oakes Avenue
Anacortes, WA 98221
Phone (360) 293-9382
Toll Free (800) 238-4353
Fax (360) 299-9208
Email: beds@sos.net
Website: http://www.channel-house.com

Rates: $79 - 109 U.S.

Channel House

Channel House sits on a bluff overlooking Guemes Channel, the primary passage to the San Juan Islands for most island-bound visitors. The inn is conveniently located less than two miles from the San Juan Island and Sidney, B.C. ferry dock. As a result, many guests stay one night and rise early to catch the first boat at 7:30 A.M. The good news is that Pat and Dennis McIntyre, innkeepers and owners, graciously coordinate guests' breakfast schedules to the ferry schedule. The bad news is that many guests miss the attractions of Anacortes and the surrounding area with a single night's visit.

Anacortes, located on Fidalgo Island, is called "the heart of Northwest adventure." Visitors can set off on many adventures without even leaving the island. Hiking trails meander through 2,500 acres of community forest and fishing charters offer up the chance to hook a fat salmon. Lovely Washington Park overlooks the Sound and San Juan Islands, the perfect spot for a sunset picnic. Or drive to Deception Pass, to the bridge connecting Fidalgo Island with Whidbey Island. The currents coursing beneath the bridge are named for their deceptively calm surface. Many a boater has uttered surprise trying to navigate the tricky waters.

For adventures on and around Fidalgo Island, the McIntyres have created a seven-day itinerary for guests with suggestions for day trips, all leaving from Anacortes and returning to the inn. Guests can return "home" to Channel House each evening, share their adventures with other guests while enjoying a soothing soak in the hot tub with its peekaboo view of the Guemes Channel.

Guests staying in the Rose Cottage can step out of the hot tub, walk the flower-lined path to their room and end the evening with a crackling fire. Both cottage rooms feature a jetted oval tub and wood-burning fireplace.

WASHINGTON BED & BREAKFAST INNS

The Victorian Rose is the most popular room, if only because its French doors lead to a private deck and spectacular views of the Channel and islands beyond. Its neighbor, the blue and yellow Country Rose, features a cozy window seat that looks out onto the room's private, lattice-enclosed garden. Patio table and chairs rest on paving stones carpeted with fragrant Corsican mint. Evergreen clematis climbs the walls, and a graceful laburnam tree hangs overhead.

Inside the 1902 Craftsman, there are four additional rooms, two on the main floor and two on the upper level. Each room has a private bath, including robes and towels for the hot tub. Many guests enjoy the spectacular sights from the Island View Room as seen through unique multi-paned windows that open wide to channel breezes. There's even a view from the claw-footed tub and shower. Each room has a special feature; the Canopy Room's highlight is the romantic four-poster bed with hand-knotted canopy. The easterly facing Garden View Room enjoys morning sunlight and a pleasant perspective on the garden below. Grandma's Room, tucked away on the main floor, feels like a two-room suite as it is entered from the library sitting room.

One unusual feature of Channel House is the location of the dining room. Guests looking for breakfast follow the staircase down from the main floor to the ground level. Navy floral wallpaper is accented with white wainscoting and French doors. On chilly mornings, guests are treated to a fire in the brick-faced fireplace.

The McIntyres have designed their menus to accommodate their guests' travel schedules. Because of this, many dishes are cooked individually, rather than in large portions. This also allows Pat and Dennis to focus on the presentation of the food, which they both enjoy. Former restaurant owners and managers, the couple has decades of hospitality experience between them. Pat also managed a bakery and is well-known for her baked goods and famous oatmeal raisin cookies, fresh from the oven daily and served every afternoon with a selection of coffees and teas in the parlor. For those who require coffee just to get out of bed, coffee baskets can be delivered to rooms upon request.

Channel House was built in 1902 for an Italian count, who owned the local cement factory. A decade later, it was purchased by the Krebs family. The house is known in local history as the Krebs House due to the family's 50-year tenure in the residence – a plaque on the face of the house attests to this. As Channel House, it also has a page in the Anacortes history book as the first bed and breakfast to open on Fidalgo Island.

Oatmeal Pancakes with Buttermilk Syrup

Serves 8-10

The McIntyres suggest making the pancake batter a day in advance. The syrup can also be made ahead and stored in the refrigerator, then reheated in the microwave.

Oatmeal Pancakes Wet Part

- 1 quart buttermilk
- 1-1/2 tsp. salt
- 4 tsp. baking soda
- 1 cup sour cream
- 5 eggs

In a large bowl, mix together buttermilk, salt, soda and sour cream. Let stand until it becomes foamy. Then add eggs and stir together.

Dry Part

- 1 cup old-fashioned oats (not instant or quick cooking)
- 3-1/3 cups flour
- 1-1/3 cups sugar
- 1/2 cup cornmeal
- 1-1/2 tsp. baking powder

In a large bowl, mix together dry ingredients. Add dry ingredients to wet ingredients and stir to combine.

To make pancakes, melt butter over medium heat in a skillet or on griddle until foaming. Ladle 1/4 cup batter into skillet per pancake. Cook till pancakes are golden brown, turning to cook second side when pancakes have bubbly surfaces and slightly dry edges. Continue to cook until batter is used or keep unused batter in the refrigerator to use the next day. Cooked pancakes can be kept in a warm oven, covered until ready to serve.

Buttermilk Syrup

- 3 cups sugar
- 3 Tbs. Karo corn syrup
- 2 cups buttermilk
- 3 Tbs. baking soda
- 1/2 cup butter (1 stick – slice to melt faster)
- 3/4 tsp. vanilla

Combine ingredients in an 8-quart saucepan and bring to an easy boil, continuing for about 5 minutes. Let cool slightly, transfer to a one quart container and refrigerate until ready to use.

CAUTION: Be sure to use the 8-quart saucepan. Syrup will foam to the top and over if not careful.

Cheese Puff

Serves 12

- 12 eggs
- 1 lb. monterey jack cheese, shredded
- 2 cups cottage cheese
- 1/4 cup flour
- 1 tsp. baking powder
- 1 stick butter or margarine, melted

Preheat oven to 350° F. Spray bottom and sides of 13 x 9 inch pan with vegetable spray.

Mix together all ingredients in a large bowl. Pour into prepared pan and bake for 35-40 minutes until eggs are set and top is light brown.

Remove from oven, let sit for 5-10 minutes, then cut and serve

From the author, variations of this dish could include:

Add 1 - 6 oz. can chopped green chiles to egg mixture. Serve with salsa and sour cream.

Brown 1 pound sausage, drain and add to egg mixture.

Chop 1 medium onion, 1/2 lb. mushrooms and 1/4 cup green onions, and 1 bell pepper, saute in butter till soft and add to egg mixture.

Substitute swiss or cheddar cheese for monterey jack, add 2 cups cubed ham and 1/2 cup minced green onions

Brown 1lb. bacon, drain, crumble and add to egg mixture.

Chestnut Hill Inn

P.O. Box 213
Orcas, WA 98280-0213
Phone (360) 376-5157
Fax (360) 376-5283
E-mail: chestnut@pacificrim.net
Website: http://www.chestnuthill.com

High Season Rates: $145 - 195 U.S.
Low Season Rates: $125 - 145 U.S.

… THE GOURMET'S GUIDE TO NORTHWEST BED & BREAKFAST INNS

Chestnut Hill Inn

Marilyn Loewke loves romance. So much so that she and her husband Dan designed their inn, Chestnut Hill, to provide the perfect setting for a romantic island getaway. Situated on 16 acres of bucolic Orcas Island pasture land and surrounded by lush forest, the cheery yellow inn is tucked into a hillside overlooking a pond complete with its own island, stable with resident equine Rhum and a miniature chapel visible in the distance.

While the outdoor setting is picture-perfect, the indoor accommodations are plush and cozy. Four rooms and a suite elicit oohs and aahs from first-time visitors. Luxury linens and piles of pillows beckon guests to curl up on four-poster canopied beds. Romantics will appreciate the fireplaces in each room, regardless of season. Private baths are replete with thick towels, luscious soaps and bath gels. Lucky residents in the grand Chestnut Suite luxuriate in a jetted tub bathed in the sparkling light of a crystal chandelier and candles.

Feel the need to coddle your loved one even more? Marilyn will arrange special services for guests with a variety of packages she has created to enhance this idyllic retreat. If aching muscles are what ail guests, a masseuse will visit the inn and spend an hour easing away tension and stress. Perhaps a lazy afternoon paddling in the inn's rowboat or a hike through the woods necessitates some provisions. Keepsake baskets filled with all the trimmings for alfresco dining can be arranged. If love has sprung eternal, and the time has come to tie the knot, the ever-romantic Marilyn assists with elopements at Chestnut Hill.

All that love can work up an appetite. If romance is Marilyn's first passion, then cooking follows as a close second. Menus change regularly as new recipes demand experimentation. Breakfast is served in the sunny blue and white dining room at (of course) tables for two overlooking the pond. The first course is often fruit, perhaps berries crowned with a dollop of crème fraiche or apples, shredded and spooned into yogurt and oats, sweetened with honey and toasted hazelnuts. Baked goods arrive at tables, warm from the oven, and range from "jammies" jam-filled muffins, to raspberry tea bread or cranberry orange scones with orange marmalade butter melting inside. For main courses, a savory vegetable tart or rolled omelet, filled with spinach and tangy gruyere cheese, partnered with homemade sausage might grace the breakfast china. If a sweet is on the menu instead of a savory, perhaps it's banana pecan French toast drizzled with an unusual buttermilk syrup or Dutch babies with a pitcher of blueberry and blackberry coulis served alongside.

In the afternoon, guests can retire to the veranda to sip lemonade and soak up the pastoral view or curl up fireside in the parlor for a cup of tea or a glass of wine. A tray of snacks will entice guests to a little nosh before setting off to dinner. During the winter months (November through March), guests can remain at the inn for dinner. The candlelit meals are served on the second night of a two-night stay with prior arrangement.

Chestnut Hill Inn was originally a summer home, built in the 1960s to resemble an 1890s farmhouse. It is a replication of the first owner's family home in Minnesota. Nestled in an area of Orcas Island called Victorian Valley, it is well-suited to its location. For lovers seeking romance and comfort, it is well-suited too.

Without bread, without wine, love is nothing.

French Proverb

Apple Pancakes

Serves 4

- 4 Gala apples, cored, peeled and sliced 1/4" thick
- 2 Tbs. butter
- 2 Tbs. brown sugar

- 1 cup all-purpose flour
- 1 Tbs. sugar
- 2 tsp. baking powder
- 1 egg
- 1 cup milk
- 1 Tbs. vegetable oil

Melt butter and brown sugar over medium heat in skillet large enough to hold all the apples. Add apples and sauté until just soft.

Remove pan from heat and pour apples into a strainer; set aside.

Put remaining ingredients into work bowl of a food processor, or in a large bowl for hand mixing. Beat well until all lumps are worked out.

Put apples into a bowl, add batter and blend well.

Preheat griddle or large frying pan and spray with non-stick spray or brush with butter. Pour 1/4 cup batter onto surface, making sure apples are evenly distributed in batter. Cook until edges are dry and small bubbles appear on pancake surface. Flip and cook until golden.

Serve with butter and powdered sugar or marionberry butter and powdered sugar

Marionberry Butter

- 1 cube unsalted butter, at room temperature
- 2 Tbs. marionberry jelly or jam (or use any flavor jam or jelly without too many seeds)

Whip butter until pale yellow and add jelly or jam, mixing until well blended. Refrigerate for 20 mintues before serving.

Homemade Apple Sage Sausage

Makes 2 pounds, serving 8-10

2	lbs. unseasoned ground pork
3/4	cup apple cider
1/4	cup dried apples, chopped fine
1	tsp. kosher salt
1	tsp. freshly ground black pepper
2	tsp. dried sage
1/8	tsp. ground cinnamon
1/8	tsp. ground nutmeg
1/8	tsp. ground ginger

Heat cider in a non-reactive saucepan over medium heat and reduce to 2-3 tablespoons. Set aside to cool.

Combine cooled cider, ground pork, dried apples and seasonings in a large bowl. Mix together with hands until well blended.

Fry a small bit, taste and adjust seasonings accordingly.

Form into patties and fry over medium heat until just brown on each side. Finish in a 350° F. oven for 5-10 minutes, depending on patty size.

Any remaining uncooked sausage can be portioned and stored in refrigerator for up to two days or frozen for later use.

A man taking basil from a woman will love her always.

Sir Thomas More

Zucchini Cakes

Serves 4

Marilyn serves these as a side dish for her dinners "inn" but they also would be excellent served as a breakfast side or offer a larger portion as a vegetarian entrée, topped with ratatouille.

2	cups shredded zucchini
2	eggs
1/4	cup onion, minced
1/2	cup flour
1/4	cup freshly grated parmesan cheese
1/2	tsp. salt
1/2	tsp. oregano
1/4	tsp. white pepper
	olive oil

In a medium bowl, combine zucchini, eggs and onion. In a separate bowl, combine flour, parmesan, salt, oregano and white pepper. Blend dry ingredients into zucchini mixture, mixing well.

Lightly oil a large, heavy skillet and place over medium high heat. When skillet is hot, drop zucchini mixture by the heaping tablespoonful into skillet. Cook until golden, about 2 minutes per side.

Keep in warm oven, covered in foil, until all cakes are cooked. Serve immediately.

There is no sight on earth more appealling
than the sight of a woman making dinner for someone she loves.

Thomas Wolfe

Chocolate Walnut Tart

Serves 8

Crust

- 1-1/4 cups all-purpose flour
- 1/4 cup powdered sugar
- pinch of salt
- 7 Tbs. chilled unsalted butter
- 1 Tbs. ice cold water

Filling

- 6 Tbs. unsalted butter
- 4 oz. best quality bittersweet or semi-sweet chocolate
- 2 eggs
- 1/4 cup sugar
- 2 Tbs. light corn syrup
- 1 Tbs. instant espresso powder
- 1/2 cup walnuts, toasted and chopped

For the crust

Blend flour, powdered sugar and pinch of salt in work bowl of food processor. Add butter and cut in by pulsing on and off until mixture resembles coarse meal. Add ice cold water and process until dough comes together in a ball. If mixing by hand, cut in butter with pastry blender, add ice water and mix by hand until dough forms a ball.

Remove dough from bowl and press into bottom and up sides of 9" tart pan with a removeable bottom. Refrigerate 30 minutes.

Preheat oven to 350° F. Place refrigerated pastry shell in oven and bake until golden brown, about 20 minutes. If crust begins to bubble, pierce bottom and sides with tines of a fork. Transfer to rack to cool.

Filling

Place butter and chocolate in heavy-bottomed saucepan and melt over low heat until smooth, stirring occassionally. Remove from heat and set aside.

Continued on next page

In a medium bowl, whisk together eggs, sugar, corn syrup and espresso powder. Add chocolate mixture and chopped walnuts and stir to blend. Pour filling into baked shell.

Bake tart in preheated 350° F. oven until center is set, about 20 minutes. Transfer to a rack and cool.

To serve, set out plates for each serving and create a swirl or zig zag of raspberry puree on each plate using a condiment bottle. Place slice of tart on plate, slightly off-center and add a dollop of lightly sweetened whipped cream. Garnish with chocolate shavings and fresh raspberries.

A house is not beautiful because of its walls,
but because of its cakes.

Russian Proverb

The Colonel Crockett Farm
Bed and Breakfast Inn

1012 South Fort Casey Road
Coupeville, WA 98239
Phone (360) 678-3711

Rates: $95 - 105 U.S.

The Colonel Crockett Farm

Gaze across the sweeping plain stretching from the shore of Crockett Lake to Admiralty Bay and imagine yourself in the year 1855, congratulating Colonel Walter Crockett, Sr. on the completion of his handsome new farmhouse and stout square barn, painted a fetching shade of red.

The colonel was lured west, like so many settlers, by the promise of free land in the Oregon Territory to all who would homestead for four years. This Donation Land Law of 1850 drew the first settlers to the narrow waistline of Whidbey Island now known as Ebey's Landing. These pioneer families are commemorated in the names given to each of the Colonel Crockett Farm's five guest rooms.

While the plumbing and wiring have been considerably updated since the colonel's day, the house retains a restful, old-fashioned ambiance. Part mid-west Victorian gentility and part English country, rooms are decorated in a montage of antique furnishings and assorted pastel hues, preserving a tranquil sense of time past. In the warmly inviting library, paneled in split red oak with box beam ceilings, bookcases are filled with a variety of volumes and sundry souvenirs from innkeepers Robert and Beulah Whitlow's tenure in Yorkshire, England. Cozy wing chairs virtually demand curling up next to the fireplace with a copy of Wuthering Heights. Large windows offer a view of the windswept plain, Admiralty Bay and the towering Olympic mountains.

Guests enjoy a hearty buffet each morning in the dining room, where individual tables are adorned by unique pieces of antique silver, handsomely set off by vintage linens. The walls are graced with more souvenirs of the proprietors' adventures in Great Britain, including a pair of unusual blue and white oval porcelain platters. Berry patches and eight different types of fruit trees on the premises mean that everything from quince jelly and apple butter to raspberry and blackberry jams could accompany Beulah Whitlow's freshly baked muffins and scones. A hot egg dish, crisp bacon or savory sausage, and plenty of fresh fruit fill guests' breakfast plates.

Two acres of grounds surround the farmhouse, planted with mature holly, maples and cedars. The heavenly scent of lilacs will enchant springtime guests, along with masses of blooming daffodils. Deer, quail and pheasant are frequent visitors, and rabbits make their home in the hedgerows around the farmhouse. Nearby, the charming nineteenth-century seaport of Coupeville invites visitors to indulge in some shopping while following a self-guided walking tour of the town. Hale adventurers can roam the rolling prairies of Ebey's Landing on bicycle, hike the beaches and bluffs, ascend the famous Admiralty Head Lighthouse, relive local military history at Fort Casey or hop aboard the Keystone Ferry for a day trip to Port Townsend.

>·◆·<

No mean woman can cook well, for it calls for a light head, a generous spirit and a large heart.

Paul Gaugin

Banana Bran Muffins

Yield: 12 muffins

3	Tbs. vegetable oil
1/4	cup milk
2	eggs
1/2	cup brown sugar
2	very ripe bananas
3/4	cup bran cereal
2	cups flour
4	tsp. baking powder
1/2	tsp. salt
1/2	tsp. nutmeg
1/2	tsp. coriander
1/2	tsp. cinnamon
1/2	cup chopped pecans

Preheat oven to 375° F. Grease muffin tin.

Beat together first five ingredients. Add dry ingredients and nuts, stir until just moistened.

Fill muffin cups about 2/3 full, and bake for 18-20 minutes.

Groveland Cottage

4861 Sequim-Dungeness Way
Dungeness, WA 98382
Phone (360) 683-3565
Toll Free (800) 879-8859
Fax (360) 683-5181
Email: simone@olypen.com
Website: http://www.northolympic.com/groveland

Rates: $80 - 110 U.S.

Groveland Cottage

Which came first, the town of Dungeness on Washington's Olympic Peninsula or the crab that bears the same name? To find out, call Simone Nichols at Groveland Cottage, book a crabbing adventure and head to Dungeness.

Simone takes enterprising crabbers onto the beach as the tide retreats to its low point. Armed with pitchforks and buckets, and dressed in waders, the foragers step into the icy waters of Dungeness Bay to seek their bounty. Fall and winter, when tides are lowest at night, crabbing can be done during the light of the full moon. Assisted by the glow of lanterns and headlamps, the culprits' rosy shells are spied through the waving eelgrass. Once spotted, the crab are scooped up by the rubber-covered tines of the pitchfork and transferred to buckets tied to the crabbers' waist.

Upon returning to Groveland Cottage, Simone will cook up the crab for all to feast upon. If it's summer, when crabbing is done during daylight hours, there may be a chance to dig some clams. The bivalves show up later in creamy chowder or simply steamed, glistening in their own nectar. Relax in the glorious garden, sharing fish stories and admiring the massive walnut trees while the crab and clams are cooked up on the outdoor stove. In season, guests can buy local fat red salmon or delicate white halibut to throw on the neighboring grill.

Those inclined to drier activities while visiting Groveland Cottage will also find plenty to do. Chances are the sun will shine upon visitors as they explore Sequim and the Dungeness Valley. The area sits in the "rain shadow" of the Olympic Mountains, which block the precipitation so prevalent on the rest of the peninsula. This Northwest "banana belt" receives a miserly 16 inches of rain each year (Seattle gets 35).

Plant lovers will enjoy visiting the numerous herb growers, including Cedarbrook Herb Farm, Washington's first herb farm. Lavender, well-suited to the warm, dry conditions in the Valley, grows prolifically and has spawned a mini-industry along with an annual festival celebrating its many charms.

WASHINGTON BED & BREAKFAST INNS

Olympic Game Farm, located five miles outside Sequim, is 90 acres of wild animals roaming freely. Visitors drive two loop roads around the game preserve to view bears, yaks, zebras, elk, deer and rhinos. These animals live here between shoots — in television and film.

Avian enthusiasts will delight in the thousands of migratory waterfowl flocking to Dungeness Spit. The Spit, six miles long and growing, is one of the longest sand spits in the U.S. It forms a lagoon favored by these birds along with an estimated 250 other species.

Purple finches, American goldfinches, hummingbirds and swallows visit the gardens and feeders at Groveland Cottage, as well as ducks, which paddle the creek flowing at the edge of the property. The Cottage was featured in a real estate brochure inadvertantly tucked into Simone Nichols' luggage during a visit to Sequim. Returning home, the brochure was propped in the kitchen, where Simone pondered the properties' potential each morning over coffee.

Ultimately charmed, Simone bought Groveland Cottage and began life as an innkeeper in 1987. The four rooms and detached cottage have undergone facelifts over the years, and each now has its own bath. The Happy Room will please its residents with an enormous deck overlooking the gardens and tranquil fields beyond. Mr. Seal's Room (the original owner of the home) now coddles guests with a six-foot jetted tub. The French Room pays tribute to Simone's heritage and the Waterfall Room offers a king-size bed where boarders can awake refreshed to view the sunrise from its east-facing windows. The Secret Room will cloak guests in privacy, sheltered by the orchard.

THE GOURMET'S GUIDE TO NORTHWEST BED & BREAKFAST INNS

The day begins with coffee and tea delivered to guest rooms. Breakfast is served in the pale green dining room, its walls adorned with Simone's colorful collection of porcelain plates. Five-grain cereal gets things off to a hearty start, fresh berries adding a bright contrast. Local eggs are used to great effect, the dungeness crab quiche being one favorite. Scones and muffins accompany, and perhaps a fruit cobbler will follow. Picnics and box lunches filled with takeaway treats are available for the daytime sojourner.

Simone's cooking talents have led her in new directions. The Cottage's Great Room, once operated as a country store, now hosts groups up to 40 for special dinners. Boasting the original river rock fireplace, 12-foot ceilings and decorative stained glass doors, the Great Room is available to groups for meetings, receptions and workshops. Simone also recommends the room for family reunions, when the whole of Groveland Cottage can be booked and additional family members put up at some of the 20 vacation properties she represents in the area.

Groveland Cottage Crabbing Adventures Adventures include two nights lodging, two breakfasts, one crab dinner for two and all necessary gear- waders, pitchforks, buckets, lanterns, etc. Licenses can be obtained by Groveland Cottage on your behalf; residents of Washington State will pay 5.00 for an annual license, non-residents get a three-day license for 6.00.

In-season rates (May 15 – October 15) are 240.00-300.00 for two, depending upon room selection. Off-season, 220.00 – 270.00.

Dungeness Crab Quiche

Serves 8

Simone loves to serve this to her guests who don't often get the opportunity to have our wonderful Dungeness crab.

- 1/2 lb. chanterelles, cleaned, trimmed and coarsely chopped
- 4 shallots, minced
- 1 Tbs. butter
- 1 Tbs. olive oil
- 2 Tbs. dried dill weed
- 1 Tbs. freshly squeezed lemon juice
- salt and hot pepper sauce, to taste (or substitute pepper sauce with freshly ground black pepper)
- 2 cups Dungeness crabmeat (about 3/4 pound),

- 3 eggs
- 1 cup half and half
- 1/2 cup grated parmesan cheese
- 2 tsp. minced cilantro or Italian parsley
- 9-inch pastry crust, unbaked

Preheat oven to 375° F. Heat a non-stick skillet over medium-high heat, add the mushrooms and cook until they become tender and the liquid they release has evaporated, about 5 minutes. Add the shallots, butter and oil and sauté until the shallots are tender but not browned, 2 to 3 minutes. Stir in the dill and lemon juice, adding salt and hot pepper sauce to taste. Remove skillet from heat.

Pick over the crabmeat to remove any bits of shell or cartilage. Add it to the skillet and stir until well mixed; set aside.

In a medium blowl, combine the eggs with the half and half and all but 2 tablespoons of the parmesan cheese. Spread the crab mixture evenly in the pastry shell. Pour the egg mixture over and sprinkle with remaining parmesan cheese.

Bake until a knife inserted into the quiche comes out clean, about 35 to 40 minutes. Remove from the oven, sprinkle with cilantro or parsley, and let sit 5 minutes before cutting to serve.

Rogue River Special

Serves 6 to 8

Simone's friends Kathy and Dan introduced her to this delicious breakfast on a rafting trip down the Rogue River in Oregon. This recipe brings back memories of waking up on a cool autumn day with steam rising from the river as the sun makes its way over the trees. It works equally well for lunch or dinner and all the ingredients can be assembled well in advance, ready to cook, in the refrigerator or cooler, if camping.

- 4 carrots, peeled and sliced
- 3 Tbs. olive oil
- 1 zucchini, chopped
- 1 onion, peeled and chopped
- 1/4 lb. mushrooms, sliced
- 2 stalks broccoli, chopped
- 1 cup cauliflower
- 1 bunch spinach, washed and stemmed
- 6 cups cooked rice
- 8 eggs or 1 carton Egg Beaters
- 2 cup grated cheese (cheddar, swiss, jack, provolone or a mixture)
- salt and pepper to taste

Steam the carrot slices for 3 minutes or until al dente.

Heat the oil over medium heat in a large non-stick frying pan and add the zucchini, onion, mushrooms, broccoli and cauliflower, stirring until the mixture is al dente. Add the spinach and stir to blend.

Add the rice to the vegetable mixture and heat through.

Beat the eggs, season to taste with salt and pepper and add to the rice and vegetables. As soon as eggs set, add the grated cheese and continue cooking until cheese melts.

Serve immediately.

The James House

1238 Washington Street
Port Townsend, WA 98368
Phone (360) 385-1238
Toll Free (800) 385-1238
Fax (360) 379-5551
E-mail: jameshouse@olympus.net
Website: http://www.jameshouse.com

High Season Rates: $75 - 165 U.S.
Low Season Rates: $65 - 135 U.S.

THE GOURMET'S GUIDE TO NORTHWEST BED & BREAKFAST INNS

James House

Francis W. James, savvy businessman and Port Townsend leader, was a romantic. He built James House as a gift to his wife the year Washington Territory became a State. A fine spot was chosen, on the bluff overlooking Admiralty Inlet, where they could observe the maritime activity in the busy seaport below. Port Townsend's location at the mouth of the Puget Sound made it a port of entry to the United States. Across the street from the James' stately mansion, the Customs House did a brisk business and Mr. James kept his eye on the traffic, keeping abreast of what and who was coming and going in town.

There was a lot happening in those days. Tall ships filled the harbor. Trade, timber, and minerals created prosperity. Along the waterfront, the streets were full of horse-drawn carts and stores bustled with shoppers. Wealthy residents built a city full of elaborate Victorian residences, replete with turrets, towers and gingerbread trim. International trade brought foreign consuls and Fort Warden, military officers, adding dash to the social scene. The railroad was coming, bringing with it big dreams. Port Townsend would be the New York City of the Northwest.

But the railroad didn't come. It terminated to the east, in Seattle. And, sadly, as the 19th century waned, so did the fortunes of Port Townsend. Mineral resources faded and investment opportunities dried up. The eastern part of the country was suffering a financial downslide too. Port Townsend became a poor country cousin, her pretty skirt of Victorian homes faded and patched.

Fast forward one century, and find Port Townsend breathing new life. The tall ships are gone, replaced by green and white ferries chugging back and forth to Whidbey Island. The Customs House is now home to the Post Office, though Customs still occupies an office upstairs. Fort Warden, rejuvenated as a public park, offers an artillery museum, marine science center and lodgings in the old officers quarters. The waterfront draws locals and tourists alike with galleries, bookstores, a wine merchant, restaurants and antique dealers. Mr. James' gift to his wife still stands, reborn as the first bed and breakfast in the Northwest.

The James House has been meticulously maintained, its charming gingerbread details picked out in soft shades of gray, blue and red. On the north side of the house, extensive perennial beds bloom with abandon, almost hiding the Adirondack-style chairs awaiting occupants. The chairs face east across Admiralty Inlet, where the bluffs of Whidbey Island can be seen in the distance, framed by mature trees

Mr. James loved fine wood and he selected warm cherry, golden oak and dark walnut to create a mosaic of parquet blocks for the entry hall floor. Massive wild cherry logs, shipped around Cape Horn, were hand-carved to create the solid staircase. Two parlors, filled with Victorian furniture and dressed in period draperies, are an attractive spot to sip a glass of sherry and nibble on a freshly-baked cookie while reflecting on life in the previous century. Step into the dining room to admire the handsome dining table and sideboard and peek into the kitchen for a glimpse of the antique cookstove. Wondering what's for breakfast?

Chef Donna Kuhn and innkeeper Carol McGough both cook, with Donna taking the lion's share of kitchen duty. Donna trained at the Vermont Culinary Institute, owned a restaurant and worked for a national diet chain before coming to The James House. Carol has worked in the health-care industry for many years. Their combined experience has resulted in menus that reflect their interest in healthy dining. Yogurt replaces sour cream in many sauces, for example, and honey is often used in place of sugar. Guests enjoy traditional breakfast dishes, prepared with a lighter hand. Fresh fruit and fruit juice are always served. Toasty scones, fresh from the oven, and a variety of hot entrees round out meals. Donna and Carol like to serve dishes prepared from the freshest seasonal ingredients, and present them elegantly.

Elegance also is found in the twelve rooms of The James House, each offering tasteful decor and old-fashioned ambiance. Guests staying on the top floor might choose the Alcove Room, named for the charming space where a pillow-strewn day bed is tucked below a half-moon shaped window. Settle in for an afternoon of daydreaming while enjoying the lush garden view below.

Those celebrating a special occasion or just spoiling themselves will enjoy the Master Suite with its woodburning fireplace, floral-wallpapered private sitting room and dramatic, massive carved furniture. Step onto the private balcony, reached through a specially-designed double hung window, and enjoy the 180 degree view of sea and mountains. This is where Mr. James would watch the goings-on in the harbor below.

The Cascade and Olympic Garden Suites both offer two bedrooms, along with wicker and antique furnishings and private baths. The fireplace in the Cascade Suite and antique parlor stove in the Olympic Suite will keep guests toasty on blustery days. Two options for privacy-seekers; the Gardener's Cottage with it's own secluded patio and A Bungalow on the Bluff. Stroll through the garden to reach the Bungalow, the perfect hideaway for a romantic duo looking to cocoon. Remodeled from a private home, the newest addition to The James House has plump armchairs for relaxing and enjoying the spectacular outlook, garden sitting area, jacuzzi for two with a trompe l'oeil view, and mini-kitchen stocked with breakfast supplies.

When I'm old and gray, I want to have a house by the sea. And paint. With lots of wonderful chums, good music and booze around. And a damned good kitchen to cook in.

Ava Gardner

Poached Pears with Rhubarb Sauce

Serves 8

4	medium pears, lightly ripened
4	oz. light cream cheese, at room temperature
1	Tbs. honey
1/4	tsp. vanilla
2	Tbs. vanilla flavored yogurt (optional)
	Rhubarb Sauce (recipe follows)

Preheat oven to 350° F. Cut pears in half and remove the seeds and stem. Fill a 9" x 13" baking pan with 1/2" water and place pears in pan, cut side down.

Bake pears for 20-30 minutes, depending on ripeness. Remove pears from baking pan and place, cut side up, on glass serving dish. Let cool.

Mix together cream cheese, honey and vanilla until smooth. Add yogurt if a smoother texture is desired.

Place a tablespoon of cream cheese mixture in the center of each pear. Drizzle with 1-2 tablespoons of rhubarb sauce and dust with powdered sugar and freshly grated nutmeg.

Rhubarb Sauce

5	medium stalks rhubarb, cut into 1/2 inch pieces
1-2	cups water
1	cup sugar
1	tsp. freshly grated nutmeg
	Fresh or frozen raspberries (optional)

Place rhubarb in medium saucepan with enough water to cover half the rhubarb. Bring to a boil over medium heat, stir in sugar and cover saucepan. Turn off heat and leave pan on the burner until cool.

Add raspberries if desired for a brighter color.

When sauce is cool, stir thoroughly and add nutmeg and more sugar to taste.

Some sensible person once remarked
that you spend the whole of your life either in bed or in your shoes.
Having done the best you can by the shoes and the bed,
devote all the time and resources at your disposal
to the building of a fine kitchen. It will be, as it should be,
the most comforting and comfortable room in the house.

Elizabeth David

Lake Union
Bed and Breakfast

2217 North 36th Street
Seattle, WA 98103
Phone (206) 547-9965

Rates: $98 - 200 U.S.

Lake Union Bed & Breakfast

As a former restaurateur, Janice Matthews knows her way around a kitchen. Janice's considerable cooking talents are now wielded from behind the stove at her in-city hideaway, Lake Union Bed and Breakfast. Begun in 1986, the bed and breakfast is housed in a remodeled gas station overlooking Lake Union and its attendant floating traffic.

Arriving at the three-story contemporary home, guests might check the address twice — there is no sign indicating a bed and breakfast establishment. But ring the bell and Janice will arrive to open the gate and usher her visitors through the serene, walled, Asian-influenced garden. Shoes are removed before entering the inn and a thick, white carpet cushions footsteps once inside.

Striking, Asian-influenced decor in shades of taupe, black and ivory creates an attractive backdrop to the non-stop view from the living room. Lake Union is full of shipyards and marinas, and boat traffic is constant and varied. Houseboat communities clustered along the eastern shore of the lake provide a unique display of architectural styles. Seaplanes glide by, landing and taking off from the south end of the lake. A terrific deck, with cushioned benches lining the perimeter, entices guests outdoors to revel in the view.

WASHINGTON BED & BREAKFAST INNS

In the summer months, a festive atmosphere reigns when Janice fires up the barbecue on the deck and grills freshly-caught salmon for her guests. These Northwest-themed dinners can be booked with prior notice. Janice's passion for cooking has taken her around the world and classes at The Oriental in Bangkok and The Cordon Bleu in Paris, as well as studies in Mexico and Sweden have contributed to her eclectic style. Janice makes breakfast a special occasion, serving each course on different china while guests sip fruit juice from Baccarat crystal. Dining areas are scattered through the main floor living/dining area so guests can socialize with others or enjoy their first cup of coffee and the newspaper in solitude. Guests may also choose to dine in their robes if they wish — Janice encourages her guests to be comfortable and relaxed during their stay.

Guests who come to the Lake Union Bed and Breakfast have three lodging options — two rooms, and a penthouse suite. Attractively decorated in neutral tones, each room coddles guests in a queen-size feather bed decked out in Janice's trademark freshly-ironed and scented sheets. The main floor room has a sauna in its private bath while the upstairs space enjoys a lake view. The luxurious suite has its own solarium with heated marble floors, allowing guests to step outside year 'round. The bathroom boasts heated floors too, along with a south-facing view of Lake Union from the jacuzzi tub.

Janice has two additional options available outside the inn. A two-bedroom apartment complete with kitchen is across the street and available to groups and families or, spend the night aboard a yacht in a private stateroom. Janice can book these accommodations for guests as well as booking restaurant reservations, transportation and other amenities like flowers and gift baskets. Janice sees herself as a concierge as well as innkeeper and likes to keep things personal by doing everything herself.

THE GOURMET'S GUIDE TO NORTHWEST BED & BREAKFAST INNS

Lake Union's in-city location makes many of Seattle's attractions very accessible. A portion of the Burke-Gilman trail passes just below the inn, offering a great path for walking, running, biking or rollerblading. Gas Works Park is a brisk walk away and a choice lakeside location for kite-flying or picnicking. Funky Fremont, the self-proclaimed "center of the world" is nearby, a unique neighborhood of hip city dwellers and throwback hippies, several good restaurants and entertaining shopping at witty boutiques, a weekend craft market and one of the city's favorite junk stores. Seattle Center, home of the 1962 World's Fair and the Space Needle, is a ten-minute drive away while bustling downtown Seattle is just fifteen minutes by car.

There is more simplicity in the man who eats caviar on impulse than in the man who eats Grape-Nuts on principle.

G. K. Chesterton

Lake Union Eggs Caviar

Serves 6

- 1 dozen large brown eggs
- 2 Tbs. butter
-    salt & pepper to taste
- 6 oz. Port Chatham nova smoked salmon
- 8 oz. cream cheese, softened and cut into small pieces
- 2 tsp. chopped fresh chives, plus additional for garnish
- 2 tsp. chopped fresh dill, plus additional for garnish.
- 1 oz. black caviar
-    crème fraiche
- 1 box kosher salt

Carefully remove pointed top of eggs by gently tapping circumference with a knife blade until tip of eggshell can be removed, and pour egg into mixing bowl. Rinse shells and set aside.

Slice 12, one-inch squares from salmon, reserving any remaining salmon for garnish or future use.

Melt butter in large skillet over medium heat. Whisk together eggs with salt and pepper to taste.

Pour eggs into skillet and cook until just beginning to set. Add cream cheese pieces, chives and dill and continue cooking, using a large spoon or spatula to lift and fold partially cooked eggs, so uncooked portion flows underneath. Continue cooking until cheese has melted into eggs and eggs are desired consistency. Remove from heat.

Pour a small pile of kosher salt onto each serving plate and place eggshells on salt to stand upright, or, place shells in egg cups to serve. For each serving, carefully spoon in scrambled egg, top with salmon and repeat.   Garnish each shell with a about a teaspoon of crème fraiche and top with 1/4 teaspoon of black caviar. Scatter additional chives and dill around plate for garnish.

Eggs also can be garnished with leftover salmon made into rosettees, by cutting strips approximately two inches long and one half inch wide. Roll salmon lengthwise, and pinch base to form "rose." Place atop crème fraiche and caviar, or at base of eggs.

Lake Union Pancake

Serves 4-6

1/2	cup butter
2	Granny Smith apples, peeled, cored and sliced
6	eggs
1	cup flour
1/4	cup sugar
1	tsp. salt
1	tsp. cinnamon
1	tsp. pure vanilla extract
1/2	cup brown sugar, divided in two
1/2	cup fresh blueberries
1/2	cup fresh raspberries
1/2	cup sliced almonds or pecan halves
2	bananas, sliced

Preheat oven to 400° F. Melt butter in 8x8 baking pan or similar capacity ovenproof skillet. Add sliced apples and return to oven for 10 minutes.

Blend eggs, flour, sugar, salt, cinnamon and vanilla. Pour over apple mixture and sprinkle with 1/4 cup brown sugar. Top with berries, remaining brown sugar and nuts. Bake for 25 minutes until puffy and well-browned

Cut into desired portions and top pancake with sliced bananas. Serve with maple or berry syrup.

Olympic Lights

4531-A Cattle Point Road
Friday Harbor, San Juan Island, WA 98250
Phone (360) 378-3186
Fax (360) 378-2097
Website: www.san-juan.net/olympiclights

Rates: $75 - 110 U.S.

Olympic Lights

Olympic Lights is the result of a simple twist of fate, kismet, serendipity or whatever might define those instantaneous decisions that change lives forever. Christian and Lea Andrade made a decision like that after visiting San Juan Island in May of 1985. On their return trip, these confirmed San Franciscans, happy in their lives and work in the city by the bay, realized they had fallen in love with the island and decided to return on a permanent basis.

One month later, they returned to the island and found the perfect location for their new livelihood as innkeepers, the Old Johnson Farmhouse. By November of the same year, the Andrades moved into the farmhouse and began life anew as island residents.

The Old Johnson Farmhouse stands at the center of what was a 320-acre parcel, farmed by Andrew Johnson and his family. Originally called a ranch, once upon a time the land supported cattle and sheep, as well as the entire Johnson family. They essentially were self-sustaining, growing or raising most everything they needed for survival.

The land has been broken up into smaller parcels, but a rural, prairie-like feeling remains. Viewed from Cattle Point Road, the farmhouse, surrounded by waving grasses and a sea of wildflowers, looks tiny, dwarfed by the immense Olympic mountains to the west and the surrounding open fields. But drive down the narrow, one-lane road and through the gate to the buttercup-yellow Victorian farmhouse, and it is apparent this was the home of a prosperous farmer. A few traces of the old farm endure- hollyhocks climb the rusty red sides of the worn barn and milk shed, creating instant country ambiance. Cheerful poppies and bright wildflowers fill the beds around the 1895 farmhouse.

The Olympic Mountains, blocking winds and rain from the Pacific Ocean, account for the mild climate throughout the San Juan Islands. At Olympic Lights, it means that guests can spend lots of time outdoors enjoying the spectacular scenery. Guests have been known to plant themselves in Adirondack chairs in the garden and gaze for hours at the dazzling scenery. The air is so fresh and the light so clear, the spirit is instantly refreshed.

Nearby, the chicken pen houses the resident hens who provide honest to goodness farm-fresh eggs for Lea Andrade's breakfasts. The picture window in the big farm kitchen frames a view of the garden where vegetables and herbs grow, soon to become part of a hearty start to the day. The islands produce bushels of fresh fruit and berries. These are served in their own simple glory, or in refreshing fruit smoothies. Pecan bran muffins or Lea's famous buttermilk biscuits round out the menu.

"There are no 'have tos' here," says Lea. While activities abound in the area, guests can also quietly ponder the wonders of nature watching the sun set and the moon rise. This is a place to renew oneself. There's a story about Andrew Johnson being so successful that he was able to help his neighbors start or maintain farms. Just before he died, he burned all the notes signed by those owing him money. That generous spirit lives on at Olympic Lights.

A hen is only an egg's way of making another egg.

Samuel Butler

Buttermilk Biscuits

Yields 24 - 2" Biscuits

This is Olympic Lights' most-requested recipe. Lea uses a heart-shaped cookie cutter to shape her biscuits.

4	cups flour
2	tsp. salt
4	tsp. baking powder
4	Tbs. sugar
1	tsp. baking soda
10	Tbs. butter
1-1/2	cups buttermilk

Preheat oven to 450° F. Sift dry ingredients together in a large bowl. Using a pastry cutter, or two knives, cut in the butter until well blended.

Add the buttermilk and gently mix in.

Turn dough onto floured surface and gently pat dough 1/2" thick. Cut out biscuits with 2" cutter.

Knead scrap dough from cutting together and cut out biscuits until all dough is used.

Bake in top third of the oven for 10-12 minutes, until golden. Serve warm with butter and jam

---

Bread deals with living things, with giving life,
with growth, with the seed, the grain that nurtures.
It is not coincidence that we say bread is the staff of life.

Lionel Poilane

Oregano Eggs

Serves 6

Fresh oregano may be substituted for the dry in this recipe. Use double the amount called for, or substitute the oregano with your favorite herb, fresh or dry.

- 4 eggs
- 3 Tbs. flour
- 1-1/4 tsp. oregano
- 2 cups half and half
- 8 oz. cheddar cheese, shredded (about 2 cups)
- 8 oz. mushrooms, wiped clean and coarsely chopped
- 6 Tbs. green onion, thinly sliced
- chopped parsley, for garnish
- fresh tomato sauce, optional

Preheat oven to 350° F. Spray 6, 8-ounce ramekins or custard cups with vegetable spray.

In a bowl, mix together eggs, flour, oregano, half and half and shredded cheese.

Divide mushrooms evenly between the six ramekins and sprinkle with green onions. Pour egg mixture over the top of the vegetables.

Place on a baking sheet (for ease of handling) and bake for 45 minutes. Remove from oven and let sit for 10 minutes before serving.

Run a knife around the edge of each ramekin and unmold onto individual plates.

Sprinkle with chopped parsley. Top with fresh tomato sauce if desired.

Savory Vegetable Torte

Serves 6

Lea serves this dish with baked Roma tomatoes; cut tomatoes in half lengthwise, sprinkle with salt, pepper, oregano, olive oil and shredded parmesan cheese. Bake or broil to melt cheese.

- 8 eggs
- 8 oz. cheddar cheese, shredded (about 2 cups), divided
- 1/4 tsp. freshly grated nutmeg
- salt and pepper, to taste
- 1 large carrot, peeled and sliced into rounds about 1/8" thick, parboil and drain
- 1 large baking potato (about 1 lb.), peeled and sliced into rounds about 1/8" thick, parboil and drain
- 1 medium onion, chopped (if Walla Walla sweet onions are available, use a large one)
- 1 10 oz. package frozen spinach (remove from freezer, let sit for 15 minutes, then chop)
- 1 T. butter (for sauténg onions)

Preheat oven to 400° F. Butter the bottom and sides of a 7" diameter soufflé dish. Beat together the eggs, season to taste with salt and pepper, and add the nutmeg and half the shredded cheese. Set aside.

Melt 1 T. butter in a skillet over medium heat. Add chopped onions and cook until onions are transparent. Add chopped spinach and cook until spinach is heated through.

Add egg mixture to skillet, stir together and remove from heat (eggs will not be cooked).

Assemble the torte:

Arrange 1/2 the potato slices on the bottom of the soufflé dish.

Pour in 1/2 the egg mixture and top the egg mixture with all of the carrots. Pour in the remaining egg mixture and top with remaining potatoes. Bake for 45 to 50 minutes, remove from oven, sprinkle with remaining cheddar cheese and return to oven for 10 minutes.

Remove from oven, and let rest for 20-30 minutes. Run a knife around the edge of the torte and then invert onto a dinner plate. Top with another plate and turn over again, so that cheese is on top.

Cut into 6 wedges and serve.

Note: After assembly, the dish may be covered and refrigerated overnight. Place cold dish in a cold oven, set the oven to 350° F and bake for 1 hour and 20 minutes or until set. Add the shredded cheddar, bake for another ten minutes and proceed as directed above.

The Purple House

415 East Clay Street
Dayton, WA 99328
Phone (509) 382-3159
Toll Free (800) 486-2574

Rates: $115 - 190 U.S.

Purple House

Pietrzycki House was once home to a pioneer physician in the prosperous farming community of Dayton, Washington. Built in 1892, the Victorian home acquired its current name when the owner painted it an eye-catching shade of violet, causing neighbors to refer to it by color from that time onward.

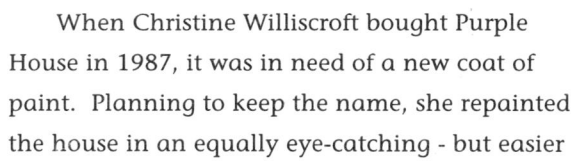

When Christine Williscroft bought Purple House in 1987, it was in need of a new coat of paint. Planning to keep the name, she repainted the house in an equally eye-catching - but easier to digest - shade of lavender and showed off the home's ornate gingerbread details in crisp white paint. The charming results make The Purple House easily identifiable to arriving guests.

The Purple House is Christine's twenty-third home. She has filled it with treasures acquired in her world travels, most notably a lovely collection of Orientalia. The elegant parlor is a mix of European and Asian furnishings, with a grand piano taking center stage in the bay window. High ceilings and large windows add a sense of airiness and refinement.

In the entry, a graceful staircase curves upward to the library and two of the inn's four rooms. A wraparound sofa, leather wingback chair and well-stocked bookshelves in the library make for comfortable reading accommodations. The two double bedrooms share a bath on this level. Downstairs is a spacious master bedroom, decorated in feminine shades of rose, with a private bath and French doors leading to the outdoor pool. A cozy studio suite with kitchenette and fireplace sits over the garage.

Downtown Dayton, just a short stroll away, is home to the oldest courthouse and railroad depot in Washington state. The Italianate courthouse with it's elaborate cupola still functions as Dayton's legal center. The old depot has been refurbished as a museum with displays of railroad memorabilia, photographs and antique furniture. Pick up a walking-tour map while there for information about Dayton's two historic districts which claim 88 listings on the National Register of Historic Places. A walk down memory lane deserves equally nostalgic refreshments. Elk Drug has an old-fashioned soda fountain serving up malts, shakes and sodas. Visitors seeking more serious libations should pay a visit to Patit Creek, where the wine list offers a number of sought-after labels and the food is legendary.

The Blue Mountains rise just outside of Dayton, and winter brings excellent snow-skiing with 26 runs for beginners to experts. When the snow melts, hiking and picnicking are favorite activities. Hunting and fishing are popular pastimes in the area or head to the Snake River recreation area for a rafting adventure.

Christine is an avid angler, and trout may appear on the menu when guests gather at the pretty dining table accented with an embroidered cloth and set with Blue Danube china. Other savory favorites include an unusual grit soufflé and spinach omelets. Christine does all of her own baking, and her German heritage is showcased with delectable strudel. Crepes, filled with Blue Mountain huckleberries, boiled oatmeal with apples and raisins or homemade yogurt join local bacon and sausage for a hearty start to the day. One luxury Christine insists upon is fresh raspberries, every day. Picnic baskets for day trips are available upon request as are evening meals, a special pleasure for the innkeeper to prepare.

Warm and sunny days will find guests breakfasting poolside. Two dozen rose bushes line the pool area and brilliant flowers spill out of planter boxes making this a cheerful place to dine or simply lounge, book in hand, while considering when to take the next dip. Well-behaved Shih Tzus, Molley and Melley are on hand to make friends and guests can bring their mannerly pets too, with prior arrangement.

Boiled Oatmeal with Apples & Raisins

Serves 6

1	cup old-fashioned oatmeal (not quick-cooking)
1	cup hot water apple, peeled, cored and sliced
1	cup milk
1/4	cup raisins
1/4	cup chopped nuts (walnuts, hazelnuts, pecans or almonds)
1/4	tsp. salt
	heavy cream
	raw sugar and cinnamon, vanilla sugar or maple sugar

In medium saucepan, bring to a quick boil oatmeal and hot water.

Add peeled apple, reduce heat to simmer and cook until apple is glazed.

Add milk, raisins, nuts and salt and bring to boil again.

To serve, pour 1/4 c. heavy cream in each bowl and add boiled oatmeal. Sprinkle with raw sugar and cinnamon, vanilla sugar or maple sugar, or put sugars into bowls for guests to sprinkle on oatmeal to taste.

Cook's Note: Raw sugar is often sold as turbinado or demerara sugar. Vanilla sugar can be made by burying two vanilla beans in one pound of granulated sugar for one week. Store in a tightly covered container. Remove beans and save. Beans may be reused in this fashion for up to six months. Maple sugar is available in the baking section of most large supermarkets. It is essentially maple sap boiled until any liquid is evaporated. Maple sugar is about twice as sweet as granulated sugar.

"You have to eat oatmeal or you'll dry up. Anybody knows that!"

Kay Thompson
Eloise

Schnauzer Crossing

4421 Lakeway Drive
Bellingham, WA 98226
Phone (360) 733-0055
Fax (360) 734-2808
E-mail: schnauzerx@aol.com
Website: www.schnauzercrossing.com

Rates: $115 - 190 U.S.

Schnauzer Crossing

Donna and Monty McAllister's beloved pets inspired the name for their contemporary inn overlooking Lake Whatcom. The charming schnauzers are a well-mannered and friendly addition to the appeal of this Bellingham retreat located in a quiet residential neighborhood east of the Western Washington University campus.

The inn is a result of what Donna describes as "necessity, inspiration and opportunity." Necessity was three private college tuitions, inspiration came from a family stay at a Leavenworth inn and opportunity arose with the advent of Expo '86 in Vancouver B.C. Donna set to work to transform the family home into an inn and since that time has gained a reputation for relaxing and elegant accommodations and for delightful morning cuisine.

Schnauzer Crossing offers three choices of accommodations. The cozy Queen Room features a lake view, private bath and other amenities and is the location of the Schnauzer Crossing library, chock full of titles for guests' reading pleasure. The Garden Suite was created from the original living room of the home and has a delightful view of the Japanese-inspired gardens, a wood-burning fireplace, sitting room and jacuzzi tub.

A short stroll through the gardens brings guests to The Cottage, situated amidst 100-foot cedars and offering the ultimate in pampered accommodations. Seclusion-minded visitors will find privacy assured with their own lake view deck, kitchenette and wet bar. A jacuzzi tub and king bed offer plenty of relaxation opportunities while the gas fireplace lends a cozy touch. Each room is thoughtfully furnished with a CD player and a selection of music, along with a private telephone. Plush towels, robes and signature slippers add to the comforts enjoyed at Schnauzer Crossing.

After a peaceful nights' sleep, guests gather in the Great Room for breakfast. The table looks welcoming set with fine linens, china and family silver. Donna offers locally-roasted coffee, a fruit course, delicious baked goods and a varying selection of entrees. Winter guests can savor warm apple crisp, while summer guests enjoy the fruits of the season, blueberries and raspberries, grown in the garden. Toasted hazelnut scones, slathered with raspberry curd or bran muffins with sweet butter and fruit preserves beckon sampling. Main courses run the gamut from Donna's triple sec French toast (her most requested recipe) served with local blackberry syrup and lean Black Forest ham to baked parmesan eggs with pesto, prettily presented in scallop shells, to baked oatmeal topped with a "snowball" of vanilla ice cream melting decadently into the hearty oats.

After breakfast, guests are welcome to lounge in the bright and airy Great Room which offers dramatic views of the lake and comfortable surroundings for lingering over a book of just pondering quiet thoughts. Soft music and birdsong from the adjacent aviary add to the ambiance.

Those venturing into the surrounding area will find plenty to occupy themselves. Skiers can hit the slopes at Mount Baker, just a forty-minute drive away, while trekkers might enjoy the well-maintained trails at Larrabee State Park with its dramatic views of Bellingham Bay. Chuckanut Drive hugs the Bay south from Bellingham to Bow, offering several scenic outlooks and pleasant watering holes along the way. Art lovers have galleries to browse along with a self-guided tour of Bellingham's outdoor art collection while the burgeoning restaurant and microbrewery scene will intrigue food and beer lovers.

Some people are alarmed
if the company are thirteen in number.
The number is only to be dreaded
when the dinner is provided but for twelve.

Lancelot Sturgeon

Apple Amaretto Crêpes

Serves 6

Crêpes

1-1/2	cups milk
3	eggs
1-1/4	cups flour
1/4	tsp. cinnamon
	Tbs. melted butter

Combine milk, eggs, flour and cinnamon in a blender. While mixing, add butter. Let rest at room temperature for one hour.

To prepare crêpes, heat a medium skillet over medium heat. Brush lightly with melted butter. Pour in 1/4 cup batter, lifting and tilting pan to spread batter over surface. When edges begin to brown, flip crêpe and brown other side. Keep warm, layered between paper towels, in a 350° F. oven until ready to use.

Filling

6	Granny Smith apples, peeled, cored and sliced
1/2	cup raisins
1	Tbs. cinnamon
2	Tbs. butter or margarine
3	Tbs. Amaretto

Melt butter in a non-stick pan over medium heat until foaming. Add apples and raisins and sprinkle in cinnamon. Cook until apples have softened, but are still crisp. Add amaretto and cook 2 minutes more.

Assemble Crêpes

Spoon apple filling down center of crêpe, fold sides over, and place seam side down in a lightly greased baking dish. Serve immediately or reheat for later for 8-10 minutes in a 350° F. oven.

Garnish with powdered sugar, sliced strawberries, sliced almonds and fresh mint sprigs.

Triple Sec French Toast

Serves 6

12	thick slices Haggen's sourdough bread
6	eggs
2/3	cup orange juice
1/3	cup milk
1/3	cup triple sec
	pinch salt
	splash vanilla
1/4	cup sugar

Lay sliced bread in a baking pan large enough to hold all slices, or two pans if needed. Beat eggs until well blended, then add remaining ingredients. Pour over bread, turning slices to coat. Refrigerate overnight.

Melt 2 tablespoons butter or margarine in a large skillet over medium heat (300° F. if using electric skillet). Add bread, and cook each side for about 5 minutes, until golden. Keep warm in a 350° F. oven until ready to serve. Garnish with powdered sugar, fresh berries and mint sprig and serve with a choice of syrups.

Glacier-Topped Cascade Mountain Range Muffins
Makes 36

Choose your mountain; Mount Baker, Shuksan, the Twin Sisters or Mount Rainier. Or nibble the top off of Mount St. Helens!

4	cups unprocessed bran
4	cups flour
2	cups sugar
2	tsp. salt
4	tsp. baking powder
1	tsp. cinnamon
3	eggs
1-1/2	cups canola oil
4	cups nonfat milk
2	cups fresh or frozen blueberries, raspberries or tart, pitted cherries
1	cup chopped nuts (walnuts, hazelnuts, pecans), optional

Preheat oven to 425° F. Lightly grease or spray muffin tins. In a large bowl, mix together dry ingredients; add eggs, oil and milk and stir together until well-mixed. Fold in berries and nuts and spoon batter into prepared muffin tins, filling each muffin cup. Bake for 17-20 minutes. Remove from oven, let cool slightly and drizzle with:

Glacier Topping

1-1/2	cups powdered sugar
1	tsp. vanilla
4	tsp. hot water

Sift powdered sugar into a small bowl. Add vanilla and hot water, stirring with a whisk to blend.

(Muffin batter can be refrigerated up to two weeks. When ready to bake, add berries and nuts.)

The Shelburne Inn and Shoalwater Restaurant

4415 Pacific Way
Seaview, WA 98644
Shelburne Inn
Phone (360) 642-2442
Fax (360) 642-8904
Shoalwater Restaurant
Phone (360) 642-4142

Rates: $109 - 179 U.S.

The Shelburne Inn

The Shelburne Inn and Shoalwater Restaurant share a unique relationship. Though housed together, each establishment is well-known in its own right. The Shelburne attracts visitors seeking comfortable country lodgings. The Shoalwater attracts diners seeking top-quality Northwest cookery. Guests staying at the Shelburne discover the Shoalwater Restaurant and guests dining at the Shoalwater discover the Shelburne Inn. Lodgers and diners are equally rewarded as a result of this symbiotic circumstance.

The Shelburne has hosted guests for over 100 years, making it the state's oldest continually operating lodging. The inn spent its first fifteen years opposite its present location. The number of visitors flocking to the seaside town required that the inn expand and so, in 1911, a team of horses helped pull the inn across the street to join another building. The Shelburne was a popular vacation spot for folks from Portland, who made their way to Seaview, Washington via sternwheeler, ferry and railroad to reach their destination.

Modern travel is significantly easier and holiday-goers from around the world now visit the Shelburne. Four phases of refurbishing have updated the inn to contemporary tastes, increasing the total number of rooms to seventeen, including two suites. Every room has a private bath, a significant change from the Shelburne's early days. Owners David Campiche and Laurie Anderson, avid antique collectors, have gathered the inn's eclectic furnishings and decorated each room with an array of unusual pieces, accented with colorful quilts and vintage linens.

WASHINGTON BED & BREAKFAST INNS

The paneled lobby sports a large fireplace warming a collection of sofas and chairs where guests gather to plan their day's activities. First on the list is breakfast, served at the large oval table just steps away. Razor clam fritters, pan-fried oysters, scrambled eggs with house-smoked salmon and homemade pastries welcome guests to the table. The menu changes daily and reflects a wide range of indigenous, seasonal foods for which the peninsula is renowned.

These same foodstuffs inspired Ann and Tony Kischner when they opened the Shoalwater restaurant. Blessed with a 28-mile long larder, the Kischners offer up the best of the peninsulas' treasures on a nightly basis. Willapa Bay oysters, Columbia River sturgeon and Pacific salmon are showcased on the fresh sheet. Razor clams, dug on local beaches, are a treat for many. Land food is featured too, with regular appearances by duck, lamb, venison and chicken. Vegetarians needn't fear being overlooked; grilled vegetable gnocchi, wild mushroom and goat cheese lasagne and several pasta options are regularly available.

The kitchen maintains a full garden, home to the herbs and vegetables used daily in the restaurant. Ann Kischner does all the restaurant's baking and is famous for her bread pudding, housemade breads and other sweet treats. Tony's passion is wine and the list at the Shoalwater is extensive – over 400 selections – with an emphasis on Northwest wines.

Tony's ties to the Northwest wine industry stretch back to its infancy. Working as manager and wine-steward in a well-established Seattle restaurant, Tony had the opportunity to meet up-and-coming winemakers and sample their wares. To this day his allegiance to Northwest producers is celebrated not only by the restaurant's wine list, but also by the monthly winemaker dinners, eagerly anticipated by locals and visitors alike.

The Heron and Beaver Pub, just a cork's throw across the lobby from the Shoalwater, is operated by the Kischners too. The Pub is open for lunch and dinner and offers diners a more casual spin on local ingredients. Mussel and clam chowder is must, to be followed by pan-fried Willapa oysters, nestled in a bun with homemade tartar sauce or Shoalwater pâté, sandwiched between slices of Ann's French bread, accented with cranberry chutney. Crab and shrimp cakes, with rosy red pepper mayonnaise, never fail to please.

The Long Beach Peninsula stocks more than foodstuffs. The longest, continuous beach in the United States supplies opportunities for birdwatching, horseback riding, surf-fishing and long walks on hard-packed sand. Nearby Ilwaco is the place to charter a boat for deep-sea fishing. Fort Canby State Park has loads of trails and the state's oldest lighthouse, built in 1856. Another historical spot is The Lewis and Clark Interpretive Center, highlighting the explorers' two and a half year journey westward.

As hung on the wall of The Shoalwater:

Wine whets the wit, improves its native source,
and adds a brighter flavor to discourse.
Good wine makes good blood, Good blood causeth good humours,
Good humours causeth good thoughts,
Good thoughts bring forth good works, Good works carry a man to heaven
THEREFORE, good wine carrieth a man to heaven

A healthy tribute to wine

Ann's Bread Pudding

Makes 6-8 servings

Bread pudding, while traditionally served as dessert, makes for a novel breakfast entrée. Try it warm from the oven, drizzled with a little heavy cream.

7	cups day-old French bread, cut into 1-inch pieces
1/2	cup currants, raisins or dried cranberries
3	eggs
4	egg yolks
1/2	cup sugar
2	cups half and half
1	cup heavy cream
1	Tbs. Myers dark rum
1/2	tsp. vanilla

Preheat oven to 350° F. Place bread pieces in an 8" x 8" baking dish. Sprinkle fruit over the top.

Whisk together eggs, egg yolks and sugar in a medium mixing bowl. Add half and half, cream, rum and vanilla. Mix well.

Pour custard over bread. With the back of a spoon, press the bread down into the custard until all the bread is wet.

Cover the pan with foil, sealing the edges well. Set pan in a water bath coming halfway up the sides of the pan and bake in preheated oven until set, about 45 minutes. Cool.

Ann serves her bread pudding topped with crème anglaise:

2	cups half and half	1	Tbs. dark rum or Frangelico
3	egg yolks	1/4	tsp. vanilla
1/4	cup sugar		

Heat the half and half in a saucepan until just before it boils.

Beat the egg yolks and sugar in a mixing bowl until they become pale yellow and begin to thicken.

With the mixer on low, add the hot half and half in a slow stream.

Return the mixture to the saucepan and cook over low heat, stirring constantly for several minutes, until the crème anglaise begins to thicken and coat a spoon. When it begins to thicken, remove it from the heat and stir in the rum and vanilla.

Crème anglaise may be served warm or cold. Makes 2 cups.

Croutons of Asparagus and Crab

Serves 6

6	large slices French bread
1/2	cup olive oil
1/2	cup lemon juice
1	cup white vermouth
1-1/2	cups shellfish stock
3	Tbs. capers
	shallots, minced
1-1/2	cups butter, chilled and cut into small bits
1-1/2	lbs. fresh asparagus, evenly trimmed
1-1/2	lbs. fresh crab meat, cleaned and picked over

Fry the French bread slices in the olive oil until golden brown. Drain on paper towels and reserve.

Combine the lemon juice, vermouth, stock, capers and shallots in a saucepan and reduce over medium heat until syrupy, to about 1/2 cup.

Remove from the heat and slowly incorporate the butter, bit by bit, stirring constantly with a whisk. You may hold the sauce in a container set in warm – not hot - water.

Steam asparagus until tender, but still green and slightly crunchy. Arrange it on the toast.

Saute or steam crab meat until just warm, then lay it over the asparagus.

Top with warm sauce and serve immediately.

Asparagus, when picked, should be no thicker than a darning needle.

Alice B. Toklas

Turtleback Farm Inn

Route 1, Box 650
Eastsound, WA 98245
Phone (360) 376-4914
Toll Free (800) 376-4914

Rates: $80 - 120 U.S.

Turtleback Farm Inn

Viewed from the sparkling waters surrounding Orcas Island, Turtleback Mountain resembles a giant turtle slumbering beneath a blanket of evergreens. This landmark shares its name with Turtleback Farm Inn, which rests in its shadow at the foot of the mountain

Bill and Susan Fletcher, owners of Turtleback Farm, came to Orcas Island from the San Francisco Bay Area, looking for vacation property. They left with 80 acres of farmland, a dilapidated farmhouse and a new home. The idea to turn the farm into an inn didn't arise until some time later. The peaceful rural setting inspired the Fletchers to share it with others who might find the serenity of Orcas as restful as they did.

It was not a simple transition, however. The farmhouse had suffered great neglect and was in need of phenomenal attention before it could be livable. The Fletchers wished to maintain the best of the old while adding contemporary amenities for their future guests. Guests can follow the transformation of the farmhouse from its life as haybarn to life as a country inn in a scrapbook that tells the story of the remodel.

Other than the pictures contained in the scrapbook, and those hanging on walls, it is impossible to detect the sad state in which the farmhouse began its metamorphosis. The charming "folk national" farmhouse, painted deep green with white trim, looks as though it has comfortably sheltered guests for decades. The rustic outbuildings, sheep pasture and orchards only add to this impression.

Indoors, floors of gleaming vertical-grained Douglas fir are softened with throw rugs, and simple but comfortable furnishings fill the parlor and dining room. Carefully selected accessories add an elegant touch. Guest rooms have a Shaker simplicity in their decor without any feeling of starkness. All seven rooms in the main house have private baths, many with clawfooted tubs and varying views of the garden, meadows, valley and trees outside. Double-hung windows can be opened for guests to enjoy fresh breezes while curling up under their Turtleback sheep wool-filled comforters. Instead of waking to an alarm clock, guests will waken to the birdsong of the island's avian residents.

While it may feel that time stands still here, the Fletchers continue to make improvements while keeping a rural aesthetic. The latest addition to Turtleback Farm is Orchard House, a handsome cedar building resembling a wooden barn. Orchard House contains four rooms, each named for an heirloom orchard fruit. Two rooms each on two floors have private decks overlooking the orchard and valley. Clawfooted soaking tubs coddle guests and gas fireplaces add to the warmth. Cozily ensconced in this private haven, guests of Orchard House are treated to breakfast baskets delivered to their room each morning through small cupboards in the hallway. Guests open the cupboards in their rooms when ready to dine. Guests in the farmhouse enjoy their breakfast either in the dining room or on the sunny veranda. Susan has been awarded a blue ribbon for her granola and praised throughout the Islands and beyond for the quality of her cooking. Insisting on the freshest seasonal ingredients, Susan's meals are composed of produce from small organic farms on the island, eggs from the inn's chickens, fruits from the orchard and berries that grow prolifically in the mild climate. The wide array of berries is also made into jams each season for guests to savor year-round. Guests can be assured of a delicious meal regardless of the menu.

Susan and Bill Fletcher are dedicated to maintaining their natural surroundings and catering to discriminating guests. Travelers seeking 19th century country ambiance combined with 20th century country comfort would do well to seek out the Turtleback Farm Inn.

Smoked Salmon Torte

Serves 6 to 8

Luscious smoked salmon and cream cheese are layered between buckwheat crêpes. This recipe works equally well for breakfast, a light lunch or as the first course of a formal dinner.

Buckwheat Crêpes

- 3 eggs
- 1 cup milk
- 2/3 cup unbleached white flour
- 1/3 cup buckwheat flour
- 2 T. melted butter
- pinch salt
- 1 tsp. butter (for skillet)

In a large bowl, combine eggs, milk, both flours, melted butter and salt. Whisk until batter is like thick cream.

Place a 10-inch or 12-inch non-stick skillet over medium high heat. Add 1 teaspoon butter and swirl over bottom of pan. After the first crêpe is done, no additional butter should be needed.

Pour in enough batter to thinly coat the skillet and cook until bubbles pop and the underside is golden, about 1 minute.

Flip crepe and cook for an additional 10 to 30 seconds until crêpe is lightly browned. Transfer to a plate and continue making crêpes until all batter is used. You should have 5 to 6 large crêpes. Keep them covered while making the filling.

Smoked Salmon Filling

- 8 oz. cream cheese
- 1/2 cup sour cream
- 8 oz. smoked salmon
- 1 tsp. capers, drained
- 1-1/2 tsp. Dijon mustard
- 1 tsp. minced fresh dill
- 1 tsp. lemon juice
- additional sour cream and dill sprigs for garnish

In a food processor, blend cream cheese, sour cream, mustard, lemon juice and dill. Add salmon and capers and pulse twice to blend, but do not purée.

To complete the crêpes, spread filling evenly over all but one crêpe, leaving a small amount of filling for garnish. On a serving plate, layer the crêpes on top of one another then top the stack with the remaining crêpe.

Cut into wedges and top each wedge with small dollops of filling and sour cream. Garnish with fresh dill sprigs. Recipe originally published in the *Turtleback Farm Inn Cookbook*.

Warm Chocolate Espresso Pudding Cakes

Serves 8

3/4	cup butter or margarine
6	oz. bittersweet chocolate, chopped
4-1/2	Tbs. unbleached white flour
2	Tbs. unsweetened cocoa
2	tsp. freeze dried espresso powder *or*
2	Tbs. hot espresso
1/3	cup sugar
4	large eggs, separated
1-1/2	Tbs. Kahlua
1/2	tsp. vanilla
	coffee ice cream

Preheat oven to 375° F. Butter eight, 6-oz ramekins or custard cups

In a small pan, combine butter and chocolate. Heat over low until melted and stir to blend well. Add espresso and blend again.

In a large bowl, mix together flour and cocoa

In another large bowl, beat the 5 egg whites until white and frothy. Begin to add sugar, 1 tablespoon at a time, until eggs hold stiff and shiny, but not dry, peaks.

Continued on next page

Add the egg yolks, liqueur and vanilla to the flour/cocoa mixture and blend. Then add the chocolate/butter mixture, blending well. Gently fold in the egg whites.

Pour about 1/2 cup batter into each ramekin or custard cup.

Place ramekins or custard cups on a baking sheet (for ease of handling) and bake until the edges begins to firm but the center is still soft when pressed, 11-12 minutes.

Let cool for a few minutes, then invert on individual serving plates. Serve with a scoop of coffee ice cream. Garnish with a dollop of whipped cream and chocolate shavings if desired.

Originally published in the *Turtleback Farm Inn Cookbook*.

A gourmet who thinks about calories
is like a tart who looks at her watch.

James Beard

Waverly Place

709 West Waverly Place
Spokane, WA 99205
Phone (509) 328-1856
Fax (509) 326-7059

Rates: $65 - 95 U.S.

THE GOURMET'S GUIDE TO NORTHWEST BED & BREAKFAST INNS

Waverly Place

The scent of baking cookies greets guests in the afternoon when they arrive at Waverly Place, a large storybook Victorian overlooking Corbin Park. Marge and Tammy Arndt, the mother-daughter innkeeping team, bake each day, and their plates of peanut butter-chocolate chip, chewy oatmeal or old-fashioned molasses cookies are like a friendly hug welcoming visitors.

The turn of the century residence has retained its Victorian aura. Rooms are spacious and glossy millwork trims windows and doors. Oriental carpets are scattered across hardwood floors and ornate upholstered sofas mix comfortably with simpler tables and chairs. The dining room is enormous, with handsome wainscotting and faux stamped tin ceiling. A massive table provides ample room for breakfasting guests.

The Arndts' Swedish heritage is evident when guests sit down to their morning meal – while traditional choices like eggs and country sausage are offered, guests are just as likely to enjoy Scandinavian treats like fruit soup, aebleskiver or kringla with an almond sugar glaze. The perennial favorite, however, is Swedish pancakes with huckleberry sauce. The pancakes are popular outside the inn as well - Marge once served 400 at her church's Easter brunch

Harry Skinner was the original owner of the home and his presence lives on in the Skinner Suite. A handsome oak sleigh bed, love seat, library table and chair accessorize this roomy space on the second floor. Another suite, the Waverly, is composed of three rooms, with a bedroom on the second floor and a private staircase leading to a third floor sitting room and private bath with dormered ceilings. The sitting room features a window seat and love seat and the bath has an old-fashioned claw foot tub for soaking.

Two additional rooms are on the second floor and they share a large bath with jacuzzi tub and shower as well as another bath on the main floor, which also has a shower. The feminine Anna's room, named for Marge's Swedish grandmother, is decorated in shades of pale pink and rose. A four poster rice bed is dressed in floral bedding and a delicate mahogany dressing table adds just the right ladylike touch. A cozy window seat has been built into the corner, overlooking Corbin Park. The sunny yellow Mill Street Room has an old-fashioned brass and enamel bed, warm maple furnishings and sturdy upholstered rocking chair.

The inn has an outdoor pool, a big hit during Spokane's long, hot summers. Relaxing poolside with a cold glass of lemonade is a favorite pastime. Guests preferring a cooler clime can slip indoors into one of the inn's two parlors, to lounge in air-conditioned comfort. A large veranda wraps around one corner of Waverly Place, a good post for watching the world go by. Oval-shaped Corbin Park, a former racetrack, is just across the street from the inn, offering tennis courts and walking paths.

Visitors to Spokane should make an effort to visit the 50-acre Riverfront Park, site of Expo '74, right in the center of town. Several Expo attractions live on – Canada Island, the Opera House, a skating rink, carousel and IMAX theater. Just west of the park is the Monroe Street bridge, a good spot to view the Spokane Falls. Fans of Bing Crosby should make a pilgrimage to Gonzaga University where a collection of Bing memorabilia resides.

Food and wine lovers will enjoy visiting Washington's second largest city. The restaurant scene has burgeoned here in the past decade, bringing refreshing variety to the city's diners. Luna and Paprika are two of the newer favorites, along with Mizuna, a good option for vegetarians. Old favorites still include Milford's, long Spokane's favorite fish house and Clinkerdagger's for steaks, chops and a killer view of the Spokane River. Six wineries are in the area, enough to make for a full day of touring. Arbor Crest, Caterina, Knipprath Cellars, Latah Creek and Worden's all have regular weekend hours. Visitors to Mountain Dome, producers of sparkling wines, must make an appointment in advance.

Swedish Pancakes with Huckleberry Sauce

Serves 4

Swedish Pancakes

- 1 cup milk
- 2 eggs
- 1 cup flour
- 1/2 tsp. salt
- 1 Tbs. sugar
- 1/4 cup butter, melted
- additional butter for frying

Preheat oven to 250° F. Beat together eggs and milk. Add flour, salt, sugar and melted butter, stirring well.

Melt 1 t. butter in iron skillet over medium heat. Pour enough batter into skillet to coat bottom. Tilt skillet to cover evenly. Cook about 1 minute, loosen with spatula and flip pancake to cook other side. Roll pancakes into cylinders and keep warm in oven until all batter is used.

Serve pancakes topped with:

Huckleberry Sauce

- 1/2 cup sugar
- 1 Tbs. cornstarch
- 2 cups huckleberries, fresh or frozen
- 2 Tbs. lemon juice
- 1/2 cup water

Combine all ingredients in medium saucepan. Cook over medium heat until thickened, stirring occasionally.

Serve warm or cold over Swedish pancakes. Sauce is great served over ice cream and cheesecake, too!

Anne's Favorite Recipes

Coffee Cake

I am the fortunate recipient of my mother's enormous recipe file. The Breads section holds this wonderful recipe, written by my lovely Grandma Alice, on a now faded and much-splattered 3 x 5 card. It is simply titled "Coffee Cake", followed by her note - (delicious).

1/2	cup butter or margarine
2	eggs
1-1/4	cups milk
1	tsp. vanilla
2-1/2	cups flour
1-1/2	cups sugar
4	tsp. baking powder

Preheat oven to 350° F. and grease 3 – 8" round cake pans
Beat butter or margarine till soft.

Add eggs, milk and vanilla and beat until well combined (batter will be a tiny bit lumpy). Sift together flour, sugar and baking powder. Add to batter and mix well.

Divide batter evenly amongst prepared pans and spoon over each cake the following:

Topping

1/2	cup butter or margarine
2	cups brown sugar
3	tsp. cinnamon
4	Tbs. flour
1/2	cup nuts, chopped

In a one quart saucepan, melt butter or margarine over medium heat. When melted, remove from heat and add remaining ingredients, stirring well. Drop spoonfuls of topping onto cakes. Topping will sink a bit into batter.

Bake for 25 to 30 minutes, or until golden brown and topping is bubbling. Remove from oven and let cool a few minutes before serving. Cut into wedges and serve while still warm. Can freeze for future use.

Christmas Potato Casserole III (Potato Pie)

One of three potato dishes rotated yearly for Christmas dinner. My mother traditionally prepared a standing rib roast, which was served with Yorkshire pudding and, calendar depending, this potato dish. My siblings and I always hoped for leftovers as this pie is even better the next day, cold, or reheated in the oven and makes for a divine Boxing Day (or any day) breakfast.

1	10-inch unbaked pastry shell
1	lb. small curd cottage cheese
2	cups mashed potatoes
1/2	cup sour cream
2	eggs
2	tsp. salt
1/8	tsp. cayenne
1/2	cup sliced scallions
1/4	cup freshly grated parmesan

Preheat oven to 425° F.

In a large bowl, beat together cottage cheese and mashed potatoes. Add sour cream, eggs, salt and cayenne, mixing well. Stir in scallions.

Spoon into pastry shell and smooth top. Sprinkle with grated parmesan. Bake for 50 minutes until golden brown.

Cinnamon Honey Butter

Makes about 1 cup

1/2	cup butter
1/2	cup honey
3/4	cup powdered sugar, sifted
1	tsp. cinnamon

Beat together all ingredients until smooth and fluffy. Serve with muffins, scones, biscuits or toast. Keep refrigerated.

Tortilla Española

Serves 4

The tortilla is to Spaniards what the omelet is to the French and the frittata to Italians. We lived in Spain for three years and tortillas became a regular part of our family meals. The simplicity of this dish is a good reminder of how wonderful plain ingredients can be. It remains one of my all-time favorite meals, whether breakfast, lunch or dinner.

4	large russet potatoes, washed and cut into 1/2" dice
1	cup diced yellow onion
8	eggs
1/2	cup olive oil, divided
	salt and pepper to taste

Heat five tablespoons of olive oil in a 12" skillet over medium heat.

When oil is hot, add diced potatoes and stir to coat in oil. Cook until potatoes are just beginning to turn golden, stirring occassionally to keep them from sticking to skillet.

Add onion and continue to cook until onion is soft and potatoes are fully golden. Drain and set aside.

Whisk together eggs, seasoning to taste with salt and pepper. Add potatoes and onions and let sit for 15 minutes.

In a clean 12" skillet, heat two tablespoons of olive oil over medium heat until very hot. Pour in egg and potato mixture, spreading out with help of a spatula. Lower heat to medium high and shake the pan often to prevent sticking.

When the bottom begins to brown, invert a plate of the same size over the skillet. Flip the eggs onto the plate.

Add the remaining tablespoon olive oil to skillet and carefully slide tortilla into pan to brown on the other side. Lower heat to medium and continue cooking until eggs are mostly set, and center is still a bit soft. Transfer to plate and cut into wedges to serve.

Suggested Menus

Fall Brunch

Pears simmered in Cider (Amy's Manor)

Pumpkin Waffles with Hazelnut Butter

(Portland's Guest House)

Pork and Apple Sausage (Chestnut Hill Inn)

Freshly Pressed Apple Cider

Coffee and Tea

Winter Brunch

Cinnamon-Sugar Broiled Grapefruit

Oatmeal Pancakes with Buttermilk Syrup

(Channel House)

Pepper Bacon

Freshly Squeezed Tangerine Juice

Coffee and Tea

Spring Brunch

Fresh Strawberries with Orange Zest

Croutons of Aparagus and Crab

(The Shoalwater)

Vanilla Soufflé

(The Old Farmhouse)

Mimosas

Coffee and Tea

Breakfast for a Crowd

Touvelle House Breakfast Casserole

(Touvelle House)

Turkey Sausage (Mt. Ashland Inn)

Sliced Melons

Buttermilk Biscuits (Olympic Lights)

Orange Juice and Apple Juice

Coffee and Tea

Dessert Buffet

Mountain Almond Roca (Mt. Ashland Inn)

Shirley's Cheesecake

(Lighthouse Bed & Breakfast)

Orange Poppyseed Bundt Cake (Sea Quest)

Chocolate Walnut Tart (Chestnut Hill Inn)

Dutch Butter Cake (Penny Farthing Inn)

Madeleines (Ann Starret Mansion)

Brie and Roquefort Cheeses

Sliced Baguette and Wheatmeal Biscuits

Grape Clusters and Strawberries

Champagne

Coffee & Tea

INDEX OF BED & BREAKFAST INNS

Amy's Manor 159
Ann Starrett Mansion 163

Beaconsfield Inn, The 13

Campbell House, The 67
Captain Whidbey Inn, The 171
Chambered Nautilus, The 177
Channel House 185
Chanticleer Inn 73
Chestnut Hill Inn 191
Colonel Crockett Farm B & B, The 199

Floras Lake House 77

Groveland Cottage 203

Heritage Harbour 19
Home by the Sea 83

James House, The 209

Laburnam Cottage 23
Lake Union B & B 215
Lighthouse Bed & Breakfast 87
Lion and the Rose, The 93
Mattey House 97
Mount Ashland Inn 101

Old Farmhouse, The 27
Olympic Lights 221

Pennyfarthing Inn 33
Portland Guest House 107
Portland's White House 111
Purple House, The 227

Richview House 37
Romeo Inn 117
Rosebriar Hotel 121

Schnauzer Crossing 231
Sea Quest Bed & Breakfast 125
Shelburne Inn, The 237
Sooke Harbour House 43
Springbrook Hazelnut Farm 131
Steamboat Inn 135
Steiger Haus 141

Thistledown House 53
Touvelle House 145
Turtleback Farm Inn 243
Tyee Lodge 151

Waverly Place 249
Wilp Gybuu 61

INDEX TO RECIPES

A
Almond Eggnog French Toast 86
Apple Amaretto Crepes 99
Apple Pancakes 194
Apple Raisin Oatmeal 230
Apple Sage Sausage 195
Apples
   Apple Amaretto Crepes 234
   Apple Pancakes, with 194
     Marionberry Butter
   Apple Raisin Oatmeal 230
   Apple Sage Sausage 195
   Lake Union Pancake 220
Appetizers
   Chicken Liver Pâté 100
   Smoked Salmon Spread 106
Asparagus
   Croutons of Asparagus & Crab ... 242
   Salmon Hash 138
Aunt Bobbie's Sticky Bun Cake 80

B
Bacon
   Touvelle House Casserole 149
Banana
   Banana Bran Muffins 202
   Banana-Kiwi French Toast 144
   Lake Union Pancake 220
   Sour Cream Banana French Toast . 96
Berries
   Blueberry Brunch Casserole 91
   Blueberry Coffee Cake 26
   Blueberry Sauce, ... 31
     Cheese Blintzes with
   Cranberry Blueberry Raisin Bread . 22
   Cranberry Muffins 81
   Cranberry Pecan Scones 120
   Hazelnut Granola Parfaits 134
   Huckleberry Sauce, ... 252
     Swedish Pancakes with
   Marionberry Butter, ... 194
     Apple Pancakes with
   Red Huckleberry-Maple Syrup 48
     Purée, Dutch Babies with
Birchermuesli 57
Biscuits
   Buttermilk 224
Blueberry Brunch Casserole 91
Blueberry Coffee Cake 26
Blueberry Sauce, ... 31
   Cheese Blintzes with
Breads, Quick
   Apple Amaretto Crepes 234
   Aunt Bobbie's Sticky Bun Cake 80
   Butter Pecan Bread 114

Buttermilk Biscuits 224
Campbell House Scones 71
Cascade Mountain Range Muffins 236
Cheese Blintzes 31
   with Blueberry Sauce
Chocolate Waffles with 58
   Bing Cherry Sauce
Cranberry Blueberry Raisin Bread . 22
Cranberry Muffins 81
Cranberry Pecan Scones 120
Dutch Babies with Red 48
   Huckleberry-Maple Syrup Puree
Finnish Pancakes 124
Fruit Crepes with French Vanilla .. 41
   Yogurt and Orange Ginger Sauce
Lake Union Pancake 220
Lemon Poppy Seed Bread 174
Penny Farthing Scones 36
Pumpkin Spice Bread 182
Pumpkin Waffles with Oregon ... 110
   Hazelnut Butter
Rosemary Buttermilk Muffins 180
Smoked Salmon Torte 246
Swedish Pancakes 252
Bread Pudding, Ann's 241
Breads, Yeast
   Cinnamon Roll Rose 155
Butter Pecan French Toast 114
Buttermilk
   Buttermilk Biscuits 224
   Buttermilk Syrup 189
   Rosemary Buttermilk Muffins 180

C
Cakes
   Dutch Butter Cake 35
   Shirley's Cheesecake 90
   Orange Poppy Seed Bundt Cake .. 129
   Madeira Cake 169
   Chocolate Espresso Pudding Cakes 247
Campbell House Scones 71
Candy
   Mountain Almond Roca 105
Captain Whidbey Inn Granola 176
Caramelized Onion and Portabello . 115
   Mushroom Frittata
Cascade Mountain Range Muffins .. 236
Casseroles
   Blueberry Brunch Casserole 91
   Touvelle House Breakfast Casserole 149
Cereals
   Apple Raisin Oatmeal 230
   Birchermuesli 57
   Captain Whidbey Inn Granola ... 176
   Hazelnut Granola 134

INDEX TO RECIPES

Cheese
    Cheese Blintzes 31
        with Blueberry Sauce
    Cheese Puff 190
    Oregano Eggs 225
    Savory Vegetable Torte 226
    Smoked Salmon Torte 246
    Touvelle House Breakfast Casserole 149
Cherries
    Bing Cherry Sauce 58
Chicken
    Chicken Liver Pâté 100
    Hazelnut Chicken Tea Sandwiches . 72
Chocolate
    Chocolate Espresso Pudding Cakes 247
    Chocolate Waffles 58
        with Bing Cherry Sauce
    Chocolate Walnut Tart 197
    Mountain Almond Roca 105
Chutney
    Plum and Pineapple 17
Cider
    Pears simmered in Cider 161
Cinnamon
    Cinnamon Orange French Toast . 139
        with Vanilla Ricotta Stuffing
    Cinnamon Roll Rose 155
Cobbler
    Fresh Pear Cobbler 106
Coffee Cake
    Aunt Bobbie's Sticky Bun Cake 80
    Blueberry Coffee Cake 26
Cookies
    Madeleines 168
Crab
    Crab Cakes 175
    Croutons of Asparagus & Crab ... 242
    Dungeness Crab Quiche 207
        with Chanterelles
Cranberries
    Cranberry Blueberry Bread 22
    Cranberry Muffins 81
    Cranberry Pecan Scones 120
Cream Cheese
    Smoked Salmon Torte 246
    Touvelle House Breakfast Casserole 149
Crème Fraiche 162
Crêpes
    Cheese Blintzes 31
        with Blueberry Sauce
    Fruit Crêpes with French Vanilla .. 41
        Yogurt and Orange Ginger Sauce
    Apple Amaretto Crêpes 234
    Smoked Salmon Torte 246
Croutons of Aparagus & Crab 242

D
Desserts (see also Cakes, Candy, Cookies and Pies)
    Ann's Bread Pudding 241
    Chocolate Walnut Tart 197
    Dutch Butter Cake 35
    Fresh Pear Cobbler 106
    Madeira Cake 169
    Madeleines 168
    Mountain Almond Roca 105
    Orange Poppy Seed Bundt Cake .. 129
    Pears Simmered in Cider 161
    Poached Pears with Rhubarb Sauce 213
    Rhubarb Pie 59
    Shirley's Cheesecake 90
    Vanilla Soufflé 30
    Warm Chocolate Espresso 247
        Pudding Cakes
Dungeness Crab Quiche 207
    with Chanterelles
Dutch Baby Pancake with 48
    Red Huckleberry-Maple Syrup Puree
Dutch Butter Cake 35

E
Eggs
    Caramelized Onion and 115
        Portobello Mushroom Frittata
    Cheese Puff 190
    Lake Union Eggs Caviar 219
    Mediterranean Quiche 64
        with Hash Brown Crust
    Northwest Eggs Supreme 76
    Northwest Salmon Breakfast Pie .. 181
    Oregano Eggs 225
    Rogue River Special 208
    Savory Vegetable Torte 226
    Touvelle House Breakfast Casserole 149
    Tyee Quiche 154

F
Finnish Pancakes 124
Fish
    Northwest Eggs Supreme 76
    Northwest Salmon Breakfast Pie .. 181
    Salmon Hash 138
    Smoked Salmon Spread 106
    Smoked Salmon Torte 246
    Tyee Quiche 154
French Toast
    Almond Eggnog French Toast 86
    Banana Sour Cream French Toast . 96
    Butter Pecan French Toast 114

Continued on next page

INDEX TO RECIPES

French Toast, cont'd.
   Cinnamon Orange French Toast . 139
     with Vanilla Ricotta Stuffing
   Kiwi Banana French Toast 144
   Marmalade-stuffed French Toast . 183
     with Orange Syrup
   Sour Cream Banana French Toast . 96
   Triple Sec French Toast 235
Fresh Pear Cobbler 106
Frittata
   Caramelized Onion and Portabello 115
     Mushroom Frittata
Frostings/Glazes
   Lemon Glaze 174
   Orange Glaze 183
Fruit Crepes with French Vanilla 41
   Yogurt & Orange Ginger Sauce
Fruits
   Apple Amaretto Crípes 234
   Banana Bran Muffins 202
   Bing Cherry Sauce 58
   Plum and Pineapple Chutney 17
   Fresh Pear Cobbler 106
   Fruit Crepes with French Vanilla .. 41
     Yogurt & Orange Ginger Sauce
   Pears simmered in Cider 161
   Poached Pears with Rhubarb Sauce 213
   Rhubarb Pie 59
   Spiced Fruit Compote 173

G
Ginger
   Orange Ginger Sauce 41
Grains
   Apple Raisin Oatmeal 230
   Birchermuesli 57
   Captain Whidbey Inn Granola ... 176
   Hazelnut Granola 134

H
Hazelnuts
   Hazelnut Chicken Tea Sandwiches . 72
   Hazelnut Granola Parfaits 134
   Oregon Hazelnut Butter 110

J
Jam, Rose Petal 167

K
Kiwi-Banana French Toast 144

L
Lake Union Eggs Caviar 219
Lake Union Pancake 220

Lemon
   Lemon Dill Yogurt Sauce 138
   Lemon Glaze 174
   Lemon Poppy Seed Bread 174

M
Madeira Cake 169
Madeleines 168
Marmalade-Stuffed French Toast ... 183
   with Orange Syrup
Mediterranean Quiche 64
   with Hash Brown Crust
Mountain Almond Roca 105
Muffins
   Banana Bran Muffins 202
   Cascade Mountain Range Muffins 236
   Cranberry Muffins 81
   Rosemary Buttermilk Muffins 180
Mushrooms
   Caramelized Onion and Portabello 115
     Mushroom Frittata
   Dungeness Crab Quiche 207
     with Chanterelles
   Touvelle House Breakfast Casserole 149

N
Northwest Eggs Supreme 76
Northwest Salmon Breakfast Pie 181

O
Oatmeal
   Apple Raisin Oatmeal 230
   Oatmeal Pancakes with 188
     Buttermilk Syrup
Oranges
   Orange Poppyseed Bundt Cake .. 129
   Orange Glaze 183
Oregano Eggs 225
Oyster Bars 50

P
Pancakes
   Apple Pancakes with 194
     Marionberry Butter
   Dutch Babies with Red 48
     Huckleberry-Maple Syrup Puree
   Finnish Pancakes 124
   Lake Union Pancake 220
   Oatmeal Pancakes 188
   Swedish Pancakes with 252
     Huckleberry Sauce
Pears
   Fresh Pear Cobbler 106
   Pears Simmered in Cider 161
   Poached Pears with Rhubarb Sauce 213

INDEX TO RECIPES

Pecans
    Aunt Bobbie's Sticky Bun Cake 80
    Butter Pecan Bread ....
    Cranberry Pecan Scones 120
Penny Farthing Scones 36
Pies and Tarts
    Chocolate Walnut Tart 197
    Rhubarb Pie 59
Plum and Pineapple Chutney 17
Poached Pears with Rhubarb Sauce . 213
Potatoes
    Mediterranean Quiche 64
      with Hash Brown Crust
    Oyster Bars 50
    Salmon Hash 138
    Savory Vegetable Torte 226
    Touvelle House Breakfast Casserole 149
Pumpkin
    Pumpkin Spice Bread 182
    Pumpkin Waffles 110
      with Hazelnut Butter

Q
Quiche
    Dungeness Crab Quiche 207
      with Chanterelles
    Mediterranean Quiche 64
      with Hash Brown Crust
    Northwest Salmon Breakfast Pie .. 181
    Tyee Quiche 154

R
Rhubarb
    Rhubarb Pie 59
    Rhubarb Sauce 213
Rogue River Special 208
Rose Petal Jam 167
Rosemary Buttermilk Muffins 180

S
Salmon
    Lake Union Eggs Caviar 219
    Northwest Eggs Supreme 76
    Northwest Salmon Breakfast Pie .. 181
    Salmon Hash 138
      with Lemon Dill Yogurt Sauce
    Smoked Salmon Spread 106
    Smoked Salmon Torte 246
    Tyee Quiche 154
Sauces
    Bing Cherry Sauce 58
    Blueberry Sauce 31
    Huckleberry Sauce 252
    Lemon Dill Yogurt Sauce 138
    Orange Ginger Sauce 42

Sauces, cont'd.
    Plum and Pineapple Chutney 17
    Red Huckleberry- 49
      Maple Syrup Purée
    Rhubarb Sauce 213
Sausage
    Apple Sage Sausage 195
    Turkey Sausage 104
Savory Vegetable Torte 226
Scones
    Campbell House Scones 71
    Cranberry Pecan Scones 120
    Penny Farthing Scones 36
Shellfish
    Crab Cakes 175
    Croutons of Asparagus & Crab ... 242
    Dungeness Crab Quiche 207
      with Chanterelles
    Oyster Bars 50
Shirley's Cheesecake 90
Smoked Salmon Spread 106
Smoked Salmon Torte 246
Soufflés
    Vanilla Soufflé 30
Sour Cream Banana French Toast ... 96
Spiced Fruit Compote 173
Spreads
    Chicken Liver Pâté 100
    Marionberry Butter 194
    Oregon Hazelnut Butter 110
    Smoked Salmon Spread 106
Syrups
    Buttermilk Syrup 189
    Orange Syrup ....
    Red Huckleberry-Maple 49
      Syrup Purée
Swedish Pancakes 252
    with Huckleberry Sauce

T, V
Touvelle House Breakfast Casserole . 149
Triple Sec French Toast 235
Turkey Sausage 104
Tyee Quiche 154
Vanilla Soufflé 30

W, Z
Waffles
    Chocolate Waffles 58
      with Bing Cherry Sauce
    Pumpkin Waffles 110
      with Oregon Hazelnut Butter
Zucchini Cakes 196

Visit us online at:
www.northwest-gourmet.com

The latest regional information on food and wine, travel, local happenings and more.

Speed Graphics

17919 2nd Ave. NW, Seattle, WA 98177

(206) 546-8523

FAX (206) 546-4942

Email: speedgraph@aol.com

Northwest Guides for Travelling Gourmets from Speed Graphics

If you enjoy touring the Northwest and cooking with Northwest ingredients, you will enjoy these other titles available from Speed Graphics.

TeaTime in the Northwest
Sharon & Ken Foster-Lewis
$16.95

A guide to more than 110 tearoom in Washington, Oregon, British Columbia and Hawaii offering "a sense of place" for each establishment along with address, phone and tearoom hours. This guide is also a cookbook featuring over 90 delicious recipes for sweet and savory teatime treats. Both traditional favorites and unique Northwest tastes make this book a useful addition to any cook's collection. Also included is tea history, tea service and much more.

The Gourmet's Guide to Northwest Wines & Wineries
Chuck Hill
$16.95

Discover the wine country of Oregon, Washington, Idaho and British Columbia! Veteran wine country traveller Chuck Hill gives you the inside information on over 260 wineries, plus places to stay, the finest wine-country dining and more. Enjoy 28 recipes from the region's finest restaurants as Chuck salutes Northwest Legends of Food & Wine. A great gift for any wine lover.

Food and Wine Northwest Style
Gilda Barrow-Zimmar & Chuck Hill
$12.95

Great tastes from the Northwest! Some of the Northwest's finest chefs and gourmet winemakers contributed recipes to this special, useful cookbook. Over 100 recipes for seafood, game, meats, desserts and appetizers. Northwest wine selections are included for each. Informative sidebars on Northwest specialties.

Northwest Gourmet Guides Report Form

The growth of the hospitality industry in the Pacific Northwest has created the need for guides to help visitors and active residents find the best and newest places to visit, dine and enjoy an overnight stay. Our guides to the Northwest include TeaTime in the Northwest, The Gourmet's Guide to Northwest Wines & Wineries, and The Gourmet's Guide to Northwest Bed & Breakfast Inns. If you discover a new establishment that you feel would be a good addition to any of these guides, we would be pleased to hear from you. Please fill out the form below and return to the address listed.

Name of Establishment _____

Address _____

Phone _____

Comments _____

Comments about establishments listed in:
__ The Gourmet's Guide to Northwest Wines & Wineries
__ The Gourmet's Guide to Northwest Bed & Breakfast Inns
__ TeaTime in the Northwest

Signed _____
Your Name and Address _____

Thank you for your input!

Return to: Speed Graphics, 17919 2nd Ave. NW, Seattle, WA 98177

Email: speedgraph@aol.com

Northwest Gourmet Guides Report Form

The growth of the hospitality industry in the Pacific Northwest has created the need for guides to help visitors and active residents find the best and newest places to visit, dine and enjoy an overnight stay. Our guides to the Northwest include TeaTime in the Northwest, The Gourmet's Guide to Northwest Wines & Wineries, and The Gourmet's Guide to Northwest Bed & Breakfast Inns. If you discover a new establishment that you feel would be a good addition to any of these guides, we would be pleased to hear from you. Please fill out the form below and return to the address listed.

Name of Establishment _____

Address _____

Phone _____

Comments _____

Comments about establishments listed in:
_ The Gourmet's Guide to Northwest Wines & Wineries
_ The Gourmet's Guide to Northwest Bed & Breakfast Inns
_ TeaTime in the Northwest

Signed _____
Your Name and Address _____

Thank you for your input!

Return to: Speed Graphics, 17919 2nd Ave. NW, Seattle, WA 98177

Email: speedgraph@aol.com